A SCRIPTURE INDEX TO CHARLESWORTH'S
THE OLD TESTAMENT PSEUDEPIGRAPHA

A SCRIPTURE INDEX TO CHARLESWORTH'S *THE OLD TESTAMENT PSEUDEPIGRAPHA*

STEVE DELAMARTER

WITH A CONTRIBUTION BY JAMES H. CHARLESWORTH

sheffield

Copyright © 2002 Sheffield Academic Press
A Continuum imprint

Published by Sheffield Academic Press Ltd
The Tower Building, 11 York Road, London SE1 7NX
370 Lexington Avenue, New York NY 10017-6550

www.SheffieldAcademicPress.com
www.continuumbooks.com

British Library Cataloguing-in-Publication Data
A catalogue record for this book is available from the British Library

Typeset by Sheffield Academic Press
Printed on acid-free paper in Great Britain by Bookcraft Ltd, Midsomer Norton, Bath

ISBN 0-8264-6431-9

CONTENTS

Preface   vii

BIBLICAL STORIES AND QUOTATIONS REFLECTED AND EVEN
ADUMBRATED IN THE OLD TESTAMENT PSEUDEPIGRAPHA   1
    James H. Charlesworth

INTRODUCTION   7
    Steve Delamarter

Scripture Index to Volume One   11

Scripture Index to Volume Two   52

PREFACE

There are just under 8,000 scripture references (7,897) contained in this scripture index to Charlesworth's *Old Testament Pseudepigrapha* (hereafter, *OTP*). It has required two summers of my life to collate and organize them for publication. One of these summers was several years ago. Since the product was needed only for a number of colleagues and myself in a doctoral seminar with James A. Sanders at Claremont Graduate School, a minimalist approach was taken to the task. At that time I collated only the scripture references in the margins of the text of *OTP* and not those in the footnotes. Nevertheless, it took nearly 100 hours to complete the job.

It was not until the summer of 2001 that I returned to the task with a determination to 'do it right'. Armed with a summer research grant from George Fox University and the help of two graduate students, I waded into the task again. Sadly, I had 'lost the keystrokes' from the earlier version of the scripture index so our task began with scanning the hard copy of the first version and producing a clean replication of the earlier draft. But this turned out to be a task fraught with unforeseen difficulties. Even good optical recognition software[1] has difficulty, for instance, distinguishing between the lower-case letter l and the number 1. These refer to two very different things and though the difference is not significant in print media, they are worlds apart in electronic media. To make matters worse, the extant hardcopy master had been printed on a poor quality dot matrix printer! It took nearly 80 hours simply to recover the text of the earlier draft. Once this had been accomplished, it remained to go through *OTP* checking every entry in the scripture index against what was actually in the margins of *OTP*. Furthermore, it became evident that in order to 'do it right' we would have to collate all of the scripture references in the footnotes to both volumes and add them to the scripture index. Nearly one-third of the cross-references to the Protestant scriptures in *OTP* are in the footnotes. Well over 250 hours later—and well beyond the budget of the

---

1. I used TextBridge Pro Millennium by Scansoft, Inc.

summer research grant—we completed a final product that is much better than the first draft.

I want to express appreciation to several persons for their support of this project. The summer research grant program at George Fox University needs to be mentioned first. Administered through the office of the Vice President for Academic Affairs, Dr Robin Baker, this program supports the work of scholarship in our faculty. I am one member of the faculty who found the program to provide the lift that was needed. The Dean of the seminary, Dr Tom Johnson, encouraged me in this and other scholarly pursuits by reading and commenting on a first draft of the introduction and by helping me sort out priorities among all demands placed on faculty in a university setting. Mark Enos, a graduate student, assisted in checking references in an earlier draft of the index against the entries in *OTP*. And, special mention goes to graduate student, Steve Graham, whose sustained concentration and tenacity were a very significant help in the work of collating and double-checking the entries in this index. Professor James Charlesworth was gracious enough to take an interest in the work at an early stage and offered several helpful suggestions as the work unfolded. I am grateful for both his input and his encouragement. I wish also to express gratitude to the editorial staff at Sheffield Academic Press, particularly to production editor Sarah Norman who did very exacting work on tedious copy.

Errors will be found in the index. For these I bear responsibility. But a great deal of helpful information will also be found here. And for this I have the help of these my friends and colleagues to thank.

BIBLICAL STORIES AND QUOTATIONS REFLECTED AND EVEN
ADUMBRATED IN THE OLD TESTAMENT PSEUDEPIGRAPHA

James H. Charlesworth

Three perspectives frame the study of scriptural citations in the Old Testament Pseudepigrapha (OTP). (1) The books collected into the *Hebrew Bible* took their recognizable shape and the list of books to be included in the canon was still open during the time of the composition of most works in the Pseudepigrapha. (2) The Bible itself is the crucible of the Pseudepigrapha and all citations of the Bible re-appear in books that are quasi-biblical. (3) The biblical references listed in the margins of *The Old Testament Pseudepigrapha* (2 vols.; New York: Doubleday, 1983, 1985 [= *OTP*]) are highly selected; they were added to guide an initial search for scriptural citations.

*The Expanding Shape of Biblical Books
and the List of Canonical Books*

The Bible was not closed when Jews began to compose almost all the documents in the Pseudepigrapha—between about 300 BCE to 135/6 CE. The earliest sections of *1 Enoch* antedate by a century the composition of Daniel, the latest book in the Hebrew Bible. The text types in the Hebrew Bible were fluid; that is, there were numerous types of texts that circulated before 70 CE in ancient Palestine. For example, the famous passage in Ex 20:22a (= Ex 20:21b in the Samaritan Pentateuch) appears in differing forms in the so-called Masoretic Text, Septuagint, Samaritan Pentateuch, and 4Q175 or *Testimonium 1*.[1] While the great Isaiah Scroll (1QIs^a) shows no division between First Isaiah (1–39), Deutero-Isaiah (Isa 40–55) and Trito-Isaiah (Isa 56–66),[2] the order of the psalms and the psalms to be

---

1   Consult the Princeton Theological Seminary Dead Sea Scrolls Project (PTSDSSP) 6B, pp. 320-21.

2.   Isa 56:1 begins with a variant; a scribe has added כיא before the verse. Perhaps

included in the Psalter is markedly different in the *Psalms Scroll* (esp. 11Q5, 11Q6, 11Q7, 11Q8, 11Q9), the Septuagint, and the Masoretic Text. In evaluating and comprehending biblical quotations in the Pseudepigrapha, it is helpful to remember that the shape of letters, the formation of words, the composition of books, and the list of books to be included in what is called 'the Bible' were developing or evolving into a shape recognizable to us during the period represented by the Pseudepigrapha.

Appealing generalizations of early Jews as 'the people of the Book' need to be balanced by scholarly perceptions that we have inherited the book shaped by the people, or 'the Book of the people'. For example, Isaiah's prophecies in the eight century BCE were edited and expanded by Second Isaiah, and later both of them by Third Isaiah. The Chronicler rewrote history with concerns and tendencies found later in the compiler of *Pseudo-Philo*. As Daniel and Esther were expanded by Jews and these expansions were placed by scholars in the 'Old Testament Apocrypha', so the *Prayer of Manasseh* supplied the prayer mentioned by the author of 2 Chr 33:11-13 and is now part of the *OTP*. Such expansions of the biblical narrative are found in *Jubilees*, the *Martyrdom and Ascension of Isaiah, Joseph and Aseneth*, the *Lives of the Prophets, Jannes and Jambres, Eldad and Modad* and the *History of Joseph*. Thus, in organizing *The Old Testament Pseudepigrapha* I felt it necessary to introduce a new category: 'Expansions of the "Old Testament" and Legends, Wisdom and Philosophical Literature'.

The Bible is the Crucible of the Pseudepigrapha

It is thus clear that we need to comprehend a 'Living Bible'; that is, many of the books collected into the Bible continued to grow in size or were composed during the post-exilic and Second Temple periods. Before assessing the significance of the scriptural citations in the *OTP*, it is imperative to recognize that reflections on biblical heroes usually created these documents. Thinking about Adam, Jews and later Christians produced the *Life of Adam and Eve*, the *Testament of Adam* and the *Apocalypse of Adam*. Associating with the suffering of Job, a Jew wrote the *Testament of Job* (cf. 11QtJob). Reflecting on the wise Solomon, Jews composed the *Testament of Solomon*, the *Psalms of Solomon*, and later a Jewish-Christian wrote the *Odes of Solomon*. Revering the patriarchs

a copying scribe added this 'for' to make 56:1a parallel to 56:1b, which begins with 'for'.

Abraham, Isaac and Jacob, ancient scribes composed the *Apocalypse of Abraham*, the *Testament of Abraham*, the *Testament of Isaac*, the *Testament of Jacob*, the *Ladder of Jacob*, the *Prayer of Jacob* and the *Testaments of the Twelve Patriarchs* (which is inspired by Gen 49). Elevating the importance of Torah and re-living the life of Jeremiah and his scribe, Baruch, led Jews to create *2 Baruch*, *3 Baruch*, *4 Baruch* (*Paraleipomena Jeremiou*) and the *History of the Rechabites*. The Torah was further exalted by Jews, and later Christians, who remembered the pivotal importance of Ezra, thus producing the monumental work called the *Fourth Book of Ezra* (esp. *4 Ezra*), as well as the *Greek Apocalypse of Ezra*, the *Vision of Ezra*, the *Questions of Ezra* and the *Revelations of Ezra*. Pondering the one who had been celebrated as the 'perfect' antediluvian who did not die, Enoch (as summarized in Gen 5:18-24), produced the masterpieces called *1 Enoch* (a library of at least five books), *2 Enoch*, *3 Enoch*, as well as other 'Enochic' compositions. The works in the Pseudepigrapha thence are almost always exegetical expansions and hermeneutical reflections on earlier scriptures or scriptural passages. Thus, to ask if these works cite scripture is to miss the point that they echo scripture and were considered a part of scripture by many Jews and Christians. The author of Jude, for example, quotes *1 Enoch* as prophecy.

How then is 'the Bible' the crucible of the Pseudepigrapha? As molten brass liquifies under extreme heat in a crucible and then takes a desired shape when cooled in a mold, so the books in the Pseudepigrapha took their present form under the influence of scripture—deemed God's Word—and during a time of stress, persecution, and even conquest by Persians, Greeks, and finally Romans.

Perceiving the Scriptural Citations in the OTP

Moving from the perception that the works of the Pseudepigrapha are themselves echoes of scripture, we can now ask, 'Where do you find echoes of scripture in the Pseudepigrapha?' The answer is unequivocal: Everywhere!

Then why is a scriptural index necessary? As a full book itself often mirrors the Hebrew or Greek Bible, so its composition is shaped by the incorporation of quotations of earlier works the author saluted as God's Word.

The works of the Pseudepigrapha are characterized by intertextuality. The following guide to scriptural citations in the Pseudepigrapha indicates how a prior text re-appears as an intertext within a subsequent text so as to

create a new text. Thus, the authors of the Pseudepigrapha are inspired by the older scriptures, carry them on, literally or metaphorically, and shape the concept of scripture with not only new readings but creative new writings.

In ascertaining what scriptural works should be placed in the margins I decided to use a minimalist approach that marks a major difference between the *APOT* and the *OTP* (see my comments in each volume [pp. xxxv-xxxvi]). Whereas R.H. Charles could readily find an allusion to a quotation in a biblical book, I and my editorial team had far more pseudepigrapha with which to work as well as the 800 documents unknown to Charles: the Dead Sea Scrolls. A maximalist approach would lead the attentive research scholar in the wrong direction and eventually in a useless search. Thus, I removed from consideration supposed allusions to the biblical books, which were only conceivable as such, and focused attention to the passages that shaped the pseudepigraphon. There are no marginalia to the *Treatise of Shem*, because there are no biblical citations in it and the introduction clarifies that it was intentionally attributed to the oldest son of Noah (Gen 10:21; cf. Jub 4:33); moreover, any guide to a biblical passage for understanding the references to Passover in 1:8 and 6:12 would be otiose for the reader. The scholar interested in studying the biblical quotations in the *OTP* should read p. xvi in each volume; the contributor was to discuss in the introduction to the document the 'relation to canonical books'. I do hope that these sections will prove to be illuminating, but one should also read carefully the following thoughtful and precise introduction provided by Professor Steve Delamarter.

Since 1983, when volume one of the *OTP* appeared, scholars and students have asked me for guidance to citations of a biblical passage in the OTP. I did not possess a scriptural index to help them. Now, Professor Delamarter has offered us a monumental work. Along with Dr Lorenzo Ditommaso's *A Bibliography of Pseudepigrapha Research 1850–1999* (JSPS, 39; Sheffield: Sheffield Academic Press, 2001), Delamarter's scriptural index provides a valuable tool that helps us comprehend the meaning of a pseudepigraphon, and the ways a biblical book or passage has been interpreted in this vast corpus. We now have another key for perceiving how scripture was read, understood and shaped by early Jews and Christians. A careful study of the citations themselves, and a precise retro version into Hebrew, Aramaic or Greek (which may not be difficult if the work is extant in those languages) will also guide us to a better understanding of the shape of a scriptural passage (conceivably not only its wording but even its orthography).

One final reflection may also serve as a caveat regarding how an early Jew and Christian might perceive the direction of influence with a 'biblical quotation' in a pseudepigraphon. The Jews and later the Christians who composed or edited the writings collected in the OTP had a vast array of motives that prompted them to labor and produce what are often clearly literary masterpieces. Apocalypticism often defined their perspective; that is, what was written was frequently a recording of a vision (*1 Enoch*) or the experience of a heavenly ascent (*2 Enoch*). God directly or through the archangels revealed to a specific sage truths that were recorded; moreover, future actions could be experienced as past events.

On occasion the normal approach to time was operative; that is, earlier sacred works are cited by a later sage. The quotation derived from them was intended to evoke the ancient story and the collage of wisdom brought to the inspired imagination by the quotation. Thus Moses and Ezra can quote Enoch or Abraham.

At other times something paradigmatically different was operative. The earlier sage can cite a later biblical hero. A pseudepigraphon can adumbrate or complete what had not yet occurred on earth. God's words to Israel through the antediluvian Enoch can refract words delivered through Moses and not just foreshadow them. According to apocalyptic and pseudepigraphic time, Enoch can quote Moses and Moses may quote Enoch. Thus a quotation in the Pseudepigrapha might appear phenome-nologically to be more than an adumbration of Sinai's revelation. The elusiveness of God according to the Bible and Pseudepigrapha allows for the perspicacity that God transcends all categories, even time. God can thus complete future acts long before they are humanly conceivable (cf. the Semitic *perfectum propheticum*). Therefore a quotation in a late parabiblical book might have meant to early Jews a revelation that ante-dated and adumbrated what would later transpire in *Heilsgeschichte*.

In assessing an alleged biblical citation in a pseudepigraphon one needs to imagine apocalyptic time. Early Jews sometimes reversed the sphere of influence so that the author of a biblical book was actually quoting a pseudepigraphon. Although an odd idea to moderns, the sages easily conceived of Enoch quoting Moses who lived millennia after him (TMos 1:2). Since an apocalyptist can reverse the chronological relation of ideal figures, so Moses can antedate Enoch. According to the first-century Jew who 'composed'—revealed what had been shown to him—Moses said, 'But he [God] did design and devise me, who (was) prepared from the beginning of the world, to be the mediator of his covenant'

(TMos 1:14).[3] As Moses' place as mediator of Torah antedates Enoch's birth, so his apocalyptic view can also describe Herod's wanton reign of 34 years (TMos 6:6). The Pseudepigrapha thus placard a human truth: 'story' displays how wisdom and vision transcend time.

These innuendoes serve to intimate the vast areas for exploration and reflection in light of the road map of a scriptural index to the *OTP*. All who are interested in the study of Early Judaism (c. 300 BCE to 200 CE) and the emergence of 'Christianity' are indebted to the sacrifices, labors and superb accomplishment of Delamarter. I also salute Sheffield Academic Press for bringing such works to our *Arbeitstisch*.

3.   J. Priest's translation in *OTP* 1:927.

INTRODUCTION

Though some ancient lists note over 60 titles of apocryphal and pseude-
pigraphal works, by the early twentieth century R.H. Charles was able to
offer only 17 such works for publication in volume 2 of his *The Apocrypha and Pseudepigrapha of the Old Testament* (Oxford: Clarendon Press,
1913) and two of these, *Pirke Aboth* and *The Fragments of a Zadokite
Work*, clearly belong within the rabbinic corpus and the Dead Sea Scrolls
respectively. Charlesworth includes 65 texts, many for the first time in
English.[1] The net result is that the Charlesworth edition of the *Old Testament Pseudepigrapha* contains far and away the most extensive collection
of texts and the highest concentration of deep scholarship on the subject to
appear in history.

This scripture index contains all of the references to the Protestant
scriptures contained in the footnotes and in the margins of the *OTP*. Scripture references contained in the introductory articles are not included in
the index though readers who are interested in the Pseudepigrapha's use of
the Old Testament and in the New Testament's use of the Pseudepigrapha
will be well-advised to read the section in each introduction entitled, 'Relation to Canonical Books'. Occasionally there is overlap between scripture
references in the footnotes and those in the margins.[2] In these cases, we
left out of the index the scripture reference contained in the footnote. By
cutting out this class of duplications we felt that we could make the index
more concise without losing significant information for the user. In practice this means that when users find a marginal cross-reference, they will
also want to glance at footnotes related to the same text to see if they
include any further information of relevance.

The editor of the *OTP* indicates that each marginal reference is placed
'on the line to which it refers' and *not* 'on the first line of the verse to
which it refers'. In those places where a scripture reference was placed
next to a line that contained the end of one verse and the beginning of the

1. See pages xxii and xxiii in the introductory section of both volumes in *OTP*.
2. In some books the overlap is, perhaps, ten per cent.

next, we created a convention for the index. Rather than make a judgment call in each case, we merely assigned the reference to the new verse in the line of text. In practice the user may discover that the reference in the margin is actually to the end of the previous verse.

In this index, scripture references taken from footnotes in the *OTP* all indicate the chapter and verse of the pseudepigraphon followed by a comma, the abbreviation 'ftnt' and the letter of the appropriate footnote. This will prove to be a time-saving device for the user since footnotes in the *OTP* are listed sequentially in the body of the text, but the sigla used in the footnotes themselves do not identify the verse in the text to which it is related. Had we listed only the chapter and verse and not the footnote letter in the index, the user would have to look up the verse, identify which footnote or footnotes it contained (sometimes several) then inspect each one to see if they contained the cross-reference.

The occasional error of versification or typesetting have been noted and corrected.[3] Users will find the entry at the corrected location.

Users should note that the abbreviation 'Eccl' in the *OTP* can refer either to the Old Testament book of Ecclesiastes (Qohelet) or to the apocryphal book of Ecclesiasticus (Sirach). An attempt was made to verify those that actually refer to Ecclesiastes and include them in the index.

The *OTP* uses commas and semi-colons to separate entries in a list of references. A certain number of these lists present ambiguities that call for a judgment to be made.[4] In many cases we have done so, but the semi-colons, in particular, are so ubiquitous that we do not claim to have checked out every case where ambiguity occurred.

Many factors contribute to the complexity of the sigla system used in the *OTP* and present in this index: multiple recensions of a single work, the problems associated with labeling fragments, the existence of multiple versification systems and recensions in more than one language. Users will have to become familiar enough with the various conventions to be able to decode such entries as

---

3.   For instance, *3 Enoch* chapter 46 contains four verses listed in *OTP* as 1, 2, 13 and 14. One assumes that the verses listed as 13 and 14 were actually intended to be 3 and 4. Similarly *2 Baruch* 24:1 contains a cross-reference to '1 Dan 7:10'. And *TAb*, rec. A 10:14 contains a reference to Ezekiel 53:11. Obviously there is no First Daniel and Ezekiel has only 48 chapters.

4.   The primary ambiguity occurs in regard to the second and following entries in a list of scripture references in the margin or in a footnote. The question is whether the subsequent entries refer to the biblical book mentioned in the first entry or to another text within the apocryphon.

Micah 6:2	ApEl 5:25 ftnt v2
Matthew 7:13f.	TAb rec. B 8:16 ftnt e
Acts 3:10	3Bar, Introduction 2 (Gk.) ftnt h
1 Corinthians 2:6	SibOr 2.219 ftnt q2
Ephesians 4:26	3En 48A:3 ftnt h
Colossians 1:16	ApZeph A ftnt c
2 Thessalonians 2:8	TSol 1:00 ftnt e

Both of the Charlesworth volumes have been indexed, though the lists were not collated. To do so would have resulted in even further complexity in the sigla system. Instead, the indices are presented here first to volume one, then to volume two. In practice, users will want to check the indices to both volumes.

The attentive reader of the *OTP* will note that while the contributors operated within a clear framework for the preparation of their work,[5] they nevertheless exercised considerable freedom. This is reflected, in the first instance, in the various ways in which contributors make use of footnotes. Some contributors concentrated on linguistic issues in their footnotes, and their cross-references are to similar linguistic features in other works—canonical and otherwise. Other contributors used the footnotes primarily to indicate matters of textual criticism. Still others used footnotes to cite the work of modern scholars, while some books are virtually devoid of references to secondary literature in the footnotes. The same sort of freedom is in evidence in relation to contributors' practice of cross-referencing. Some contributors paid special attention to internal cross-references while others did not.[6] Even when it comes to cross-referencing scripture, there is quite a variety among contributors, both in terms of quantity and focus.[7] A few books contain only a limited number of scripture cross-references.[8] Some books cross-reference passages from the Old Testament but none from the New Testament.[9]

---

5.   See pp. xv-xvii in both volumes.

6.   For instance, the function of footnotes in *1 Enoch, 2 Enoch, 3 Enoch* and *Ascension of Isaiah* is primarily for the purpose of indicating internal cross-references. But in other books, like *Jubilees*, there are no internal cross-references given at all.

7.   For instance, the *Letter of Aristeas* contains no marginal cross-references to canonical works and only one footnote with a scripture cross-reference. *Joseph and Aseneth* contains no marginal cross-references; all cross-references are contained in footnotes.

8.   Neither *The Questions of Ezra* nor *The Revelation of Ezra* indicate in margins or footnotes that they are related to the biblical character Ezra. Neither does the *Trea-*

Generally, however, the contributors to the *OTP* were painstaking in their attention to the Pseudepigrapha's use of the Old Testament and to the New Testament's use of the Pseudepigrapha—as the 7,897 cross-references in this index would indicate.[10] The collected cross-references from the *OTP* represent a veritable mine of data from which the informed user can extract an extraordinary amount of information on a wide variety of topics.

In particular, I hope that, by means of this index, users will have a more convenient point of entry into the study of the intertextuality of scripture and Pseudepigrapha than has ever been available before.

Steve Delamarter
Advent 2001

tise of Shem indicate in its footnotes or margins that it is related to the biblical character Shem. In contrast, *The Testament of Job* is cross-referenced to the biblical book of Job 141 times.

9.   For instance, the margins of *The Lives of the Prophets* are conspicuous for the few references to the New Testament that they contain. An obvious opportunity to include this type of reference would have been at *LivPro* 2:8 where the text says, 'through a savior, a child born of a virgin in a manger'. This text clearly relates to Luke 2:12 in some way or another, but one finds a note to this effect only in the footnote.

10.   It should not be overlooked that the contributors gave painstaking attention to the intertextuality between the Pseudepigrapha and various other bodies of literature besides the Christian scriptures. It is to be hoped that, at some point in the future, a similar publication can provide an index to these.

OLD TESTAMENT

Genesis
1:1	TAb 11:9 ftnt e
1:1-4	4Ezra 6:38
1:1f.	3En 26:9
1:1f.	SibOr 1.5
1:2	TAdam 2:10
1:2	1En 108:3 ftnt h
1:2	2En 24:5 ftnt h
1:2	3En 23:1
1:3	2En 26:1 ftnt a
1:4	2En 27:1
1:6-7	2Bar 14:17
1:6-8	3Bar 2:1 ftnt a
1:6f.	3En 42:1
1:7-9	TAsh 7:3 ftnt a
1:7f.	TAdam 1:5
1:9 (0 sic)	2En 28:1
1:11	2En 30:1
1:12	2En 25:3
1:14	2En 40:6 ftnt g
1:14-19	2En 30:2
1:16	3En 26:4
1:16	3En 26:6
1:16	ApAdam 5:10
1:16	ApAdam 7:41
1:20-21	SibOr Frag 3.7
1:20-26	2En 30:7
1:22	SibOr Frag 3.9
1:26	2En 30:12
1:26	3En 48D:8
1:26	SibOr 1.23
1:26	SibOr 8.266
1:26	SibOr 8.402
1:26	SibOr Frag 3.12

1:26f.	TNaph 2:5
1:27	2En 44:1 ftnt c
1:27	2En 65:2
1:27	3En 48C:1
1:28	2En 30:12
1:28	2En 58:3
1:28	SibOr 1.57
2:2	ApEl 5:37 ftnt p3
2:7	ApAdam 1:2
2:7	ApAdam 2:5
2:7	TIsaac 3:15
2:7 (LXX)	TAb 11:9 ftnt c
2:8	GkApEzra 2:12 ftnt d
2:8	GkApEzra 5:21 ftnt f
2:8	2En 42:3
2:8	3En 5:5
2:8	3En 48D:8
2:8 (LXX)	TAb rec. A 11:1
2:9	1En 25:4
2:9	2En 8:2
2:9	GkApEzra 2:12
2:9	TLevi 18:11
2:10	3En 5:5
2:10	3En 18:19
2:10-14	2En 8:5
2:15-19	GkApEzra 2:12
2:17	2En 30:15
2:17	2En 30:16
2:17	3Bar 4:8 (Gk.) ftnt s
2:19	2En 58:2
2:19	2En 58:3
2:19	3En 45:3
2:19-20	ApAdam 3:7 ftnt d
2:21	ApAdam 2:2 ftnt b

Genesis (cont.)

2:21f.	SibOr 1.28
2:21-23	ApAdam 1:4 ftnt d
3:1-6	SibOr 1.40
3:1-13	SibOr 8.261
3:1f.	ApAb 23:1
3:1f.	GkApEzra 2:16
3:1f.	3Bar 4:3 (Gk.) ftnt c
3:1f.	GkApEzra 2:16
3:1f.	2En 29:3 ftnt i
3:3	3Bar 4:8 (Gk.) ftnt s
3:6	2En 31:6
3:8	3En 23:18
3:8	ApAdam 2:4
3:8	2En 8:3 ftnt f
3:14	SibOr 1.60
3:14	3Bar 4:3 (Slav.) ftnt e
3:16	2Bar 56:6
3:17	TIss 5:5 ftnt b
3:19	SibOr 1.58
3:19	ApAdam 2:10
3:19b	2En 32:1 ftnt b
3:22	1En 25:4
3:22	2En 8:2
3:22	2En 22:10 ftnt q
3:22	3En 23:18
3:22	3En 48D:8
3:22-24	2En 32:1 ftnt b
3:23f.	3En 5:1
3:24	2En 42:4
3:24	3En 22:6
3:24	3En 35:6 ftnt h
3:24	3En 32:1 ftnt c
3:24	TLevi 18:10 ftnt d
3:25	2En 30:1 ftnt a
4:2-5	TIss 5:5
4:8	TAb rec. A 13:3
4:10	1En 22:7
4:10	SibOr 3.313
4:15	TBenj 7:3
4:15	ApEl 3:15 ftnt x
4:18	2En 1:9
4:18-24	TSol 8:5 ftnt d
4:24	TBenj 7:4
4:26	3En 5:5
5:1f.	2En 71:32 ftnt o
5:3	ApAdam 1:8
5:4 (LXX)	ApAdam 1:1

5:5	2Bar 17:1f.
5:18-24	3En 4:2
5:21-23	2En 1:1
5:21-24	3En 4:7 ftnt o
5:24	2En 1a:1 ftnt d
5:24	3En 1 Superscription
5:24	3En 27:2 ftnt g
5:24	4Ezra 6:26
5:24	TIsaac 3:16
5:24	ApZeph 5:5 ftnt a
5:24	ApDan 14:2 ftnt b
5:24	TJob 52:6 ftnt e
6:1	TNaph 3:4
6:1f.	4Ezra 3:9
6:1f.	SibOr 1.98 ftnt f
6:1f.	2En 7:3 ftnt i
6:1f.	2En 29:3 ftnt i
6:1-4	1En 6:1f.
6:1-4	2En 18:4
6:1-4	2Bar 56:13
6:1-4	TReu 5:6
6:1-4	TSol 5:3
6:1-4	TSol 6:2
6:1-4	3Bar 4:10 ftnt u
6:1-4	2En 34:1 ftnt b
6:1-4	TSol 1:13 ftnt p
6:1-7	3En 4:3
6:1–ch. 13	SibOr 2.215 ftnt p2
6:3	ApAdam 2:10
6:4	TSol 17:1
6:4 (LXX)	SibOr 1.123 ftnt i
6:4	3En 5:9 ftnt j
6:8	3En 45:3
6:8	2Bar 3:5
6:8	2Bar 28:6
6:9	2En 35:1
6:9	SibOr 1.125
6:9 (LXX)	ApZeph 10:10 ftnt b
6:9	SibOr 1.293 ftnt x
6:12	4Ezra 3:8
6:15	2En 73:1
6:17	2En 34:3
6:17	ApAdam 3:3
6:17	ApAdam 3:4
6:18	ApAdam 3:7
7:2-3	ApAdam 3:7
7:4	ApEl 1:4 ftnt r
7:7	SibOr 1.205

7:11	2En 28:3	11:9	SibOr 3.104
7:11	2En 70:8	11:27-28	TNaph 1:9 ftnt b
7:11	2En 73:4	12:1 (LXX)	TAb rec. B 2:8 ftnt b
7:11	3En 15B:2	12:1	4Ezra 3:14
7:11	3En 4:7 ftnt o	12:1	ApAb 8:4
7:11	TAsh 7:3 ftnt a	12:1-3	ApAb 32:5 ftnt d
7:12	2En 73:7	12:1-7	TAb rec. A 3:6
7:17	2En 73:7	12:3	TLevi 4:6
7:17	SibOr 1.281	12:14-20	ApAb 32:5 ftnt d
7:23	ApEl 1:4 ftnt r	13:10	2En 8:3 ftnt f
8:1	3En 23:13	14:1	2En 33:11
8:2	2En 28:3	14:9	2En 33:11
8:3	2En 73:8	14:9	TSim 6:3 ftnt b
8:4	2En 73:8	14:13	2En 21:3 ftnt e
8:6	SibOr 1.230	14:18	TLevi 8:4 ftnt c
8:11	2Bar 77:24	14:18-20	TReu 6:11 ftnt e
8:14	2En 73:6 ftnt e	14:20	TLevi 9:3 ftnt b
8:15 (LXX)	ApDan 13:8 ftnt g	15:1	ApAb 9:1
8:21	TAb 16:8 ftnt b	15:1	2Bar 3:1 ftnt 3a
9:1	SibOr 1.272	15:2 (LXX)	TAb 1:7 ftnt h
9:1-3	ApAdam 3:8	15:2 (LXX)	TAb 2:1 ftnt a
9:4	1En 7:4	15:2 (LXX)	TAb 4:6 ftnt c
9:5	2En 58:4	15:3	ApAb 32:2 ftnt a
9:11	SibOr 1.318	15:5	4Ezra 3:15
9:13	3En 22C:4	15:5	GkApEzra 2:32
9:14	3En 21:4	15:5	ApAb 20:3
9:18-19	ApAdam 4:1	15:8	2Bar 3:1 ftnt 3a
9:20-27	ApAdam 4:5 ftnt b	15:8 (LXX)	TAb 1:7 ftnt h
9:28	2En 73:9	15:8 (LXX)	TAb 4:6 ftnt c
10:1	3En 17:8 ftnt r	15:9f.	ApAb 9:5
10:1f.	3En 2:3	15:9f.	ApAb 12:6
10:1f (LXX)	ApAdam 4:9	15:11	ApAb 13:3
10:8	3En 45:3	15:12	4Ezra 3:15
10:16	TSol 26:1f.	15:13	ApAb 32:2
10:21-23	3Bar 3:8 (Gk.) ftnt h	15:14	ApAb 32:4 ftnt b
10:32	3En 17:8 ftnt r	15:15	2Bar 3:7
11:1	2En 70:25	15:15	2Bar 44:3
11:1f.	3Bar 3:5 ftnt e	15:17	4Ezra 3:15
11:1-9	SibOr 3.98	15:17	ApAb 15:1
11:1-9	SibOr 3.218	15:18	ApEl 2:44
11:1-9	SibOr 8.4	16:1f.	ApDan 1:2
11:1-9	SibOr 11.10f.	16:7	TJos 6:2 ftnt a
11:1-9	TJud 25:3 ftnt a	16:11	3En 45:3
11:1-9	3Bar 2:7 ftnt l	17:1	3En 42:6
11:1-9	3En 45:3 ftnt l	17:1f.	TIsaac 8:5
11:7	3En 30:2 ftnt e	17:5	3En 45:3
11:7f.	3Bar 3:6 ftnt g	17:5 (LXX)	TAb rec. B 2:9 ftnt c
11:9	3En 45:3	17:19	3En 45:3

Genesis (cont.)

18:1 (LXX)	TAb 1:2 ftnt a
18:1f.	ApZeph 9:5
18:1f.	2En 1:4 ftnt j
18:1f.	TAb 2:2 ftnt b
18:1-8	TAb rec. A 6:4
18:1-8	TAb rec. B 2:10
18:1-8	TAb rec. B 6:10
18:2	ApAdam 2:1
18:2	2En 1:7 ftnt u
18:2	TAb 3:6 ftnt b
18:8	TJob 13:2 ftnt b
18:11-14	TAb rec. A 8:6
18:22-25	2Bar 14:7
18:22-33	ApSedr 12:5
18:22-33	TAb 14:5 ftnt b
18:23	4Ezra 7:106
18:23-33	ApEl 5:12 ftnt f2
18:27	ApAb 20:5
18:30	ApAb 20:6
19:1	TNaph 3:4
19:1	TAsh 7:1
19:11	3Bar 3:8 (Gk.) ftnt h
19:12f.	TAb rec. B 6:13
19:19	2Bar 28:6
19:24	4Ezra 2:8
19:24	GkApEzra 2:19
19:24	TZeb 10:3 ftnt b
19:24-28	ApAdam 5:10 ftnt c
20:31	TJob 1:6 ftnt m
22:1	TJos 2:7
22:1f.	TIsaac 8:4
22:15-18	TJos 6:6 ftnt b
22:16-18	TMos 3:9
22:17	TAb rec. A 3:6
22:17	TAb rec. A 8:6
22:17	TAb 1:5 ftnt e
22:17	TAb 4:11 ftnt f
22:17 (LXX)	GkApEzra 3:10
24:1f.	GkApEzra 2:16
24:3	TJob 45:3 ftnt b
24:37	TJob 45:3 ftnt b
25:20	ApAb 2:3 ftnt a
25:26	3En 45:3
26:34f.	TJob 45:3 ftnt b
27:1f.	TIsaac 2:20
27:1f.	TJud 2:2 ftnt a
27:1f.	TJud 9:1 ftnt a
27:1f.	TLevi 9:2 ftnt a
27:4	2En 56:1
27:46–28:1	TJob 45:3 ftnt b
28:1f.	TLevi 9:3 ftnt b
28:10-17	TLevi 8:1 ftnt a
28:10-22	TLevi 9:3
28:10-22	TIsaac 2:22
28:12	TLevi 2:5
28:12	ApEl 5:39 ftnt s3
28:12	3En 22 rec. B:1 ftnt b
28:12f.	2En 1:5 ftnt p
28:17	TLevi 5:1
29:33	TSim 2:2
29:35	TJud 1:3
30:1-24	TIss 1:3
30:8	TNaph 1:6
30:9-13	TNaph 1:11 ftnt c
30:20	TZeb 1:3
30:22	TIss 2:2 ftnt a
30:25–31:16	TZeb 1:3 ftnt a
30:37 (LXX)	GkApEzra 1:3
32:1f.	3En 1:6 ftnt i
32:13	GkApEzra 2:32
32:25	2En 1:4 ftnt j
34:1-31	TLevi 2:3
34:25-31	TLevi 6:5f.
35:9	TLevi 8:1 ftnt a
35:11-15	TJac 7:7
35:16-20	TBenj 1:3
35:18	TBenj 1:6 ftnt a
35:22	TReu 3:11
36:1f.	TJud 9:1 ftnt a
36:33f.	TJob 1:1
37:1f.	TZeb 1:7 ftnt b
37:1f.	TGad 1:4 ftnt a
37:9-11	TNaph 5:1-3 ftnt b
37:20	TZeb 3:3
37:21f.	TZeb 2:7
37:22	TZeb 4:4
37:25-28	TSim 2:9
37:26	TGad 2:3 ftnt a
37:26f.	TZeb 1:7 ftnt b
37:29	TZeb 4:4
37:31	TBenj 2:2
37:32	TZeb 4:10
37:39-45	TJos 1:1 ftnt a
38:1f.	TJud 13:1 ftnt a
38:1-5	TJud 8:1

38:6-11	TJud 10:2	1:11	SibOr 5.182
38:12	TJud 13:3 ftnt b	1:14	2Bar 58:2
38:12-26	TJud 12:1	1:16	ApEl 2:37 ftnt s2
38:27-30	TJud 12:8 ftnt a	2:5-10	SibOr 3.253
39:1–ch. 41	SibOr 11.28	2:10	2Bar 59:1
39:12-20	TJos 8:2	3:4	4Ezra 14:2
39:66	TSim 5:1	3:14	SibOr 1.137f.
40:11	3En 45:5 ftnt t	3:14	SibOr 5.173 ftnt q2
41:38	TSim 4:4	3:14	3En 42:2
41:45 (LXX)	ApEl 2:46 ftnt i3	3:19	GkApEzra 7:11 ftnt d
42:25-35	TJos 17:4	4:14	2Bar 59:1
42:36	2En 1a:1 ftnt d	6:8	TAb rec. A 8:5
43:20 (LXX)	2En 21:4 ftnt g	6:16-25	TLevi 12:1f.
43:30	TZeb 8:4	6:20	TLevi 12:4
44:20	TBenj 1:6 ftnt a	7:1f.–ch. 11	TSol 25:4
45:1-15	TZeb 8:4	7:3	ApAdam 6:5
46:1-7	TJac 1:11	7:11-13	TSol 25:4
46:1-7	TJac 3:6	7:14–12:34	SibOr 11.31
46:15	TJob 1:6 ftnt m	7:19f.	ApEl 2:44
46:20	ApEl 2:46 ftnt i3	9:24	3En 42:3
46:30	TJac 1:13	10:13	3En 23:3
46:34	TJac 2:1	10:21-23	SibOr 12.215
47:9	2Bar 16:1	10:21-23	TSim 8:3
47:11	TSim 4:7	11:1-11	TSim 8:3 ftnt a
47:27-31	TJac 4:1	13:2	2En 2:2 ftnt g
48:1f.	TJac 4:14	13:9	ApEl 1:9 ftnt e2
48:7	TJos 20:3 ftnt a	13:19	TJos 20:2
48:22	TJud 3:1 ftnt a	13:21	SibOr 3.250
49:1f.	TReu 1:2 ftnt b	13:21	4Ezra 1:13
49:1f.	TLevi 6:6 ftnt c	13:21f.	ApEl 5:5
49:7	TSim 5:6	13:21f.	TSol 23:2
49:8-10	TJud 1:6	14:1–ch. 15	SibOr 11.34
49:9	ApEl 2:6 ftnt p	14:2	4Ezra 1:10
49:10	TJud 22:3	14:8f.	TSol 25:5
49:13	TZeb 5:5	14:19f.	TSol 23:2
49:15	TIss 3:1	14:21	3En 23:2
49:15	TIss 5:3	14:21-23	TSol 25:7
49:17	ApDan 8:2 ftnt b	14:25	SibOr 3.709
49:21	TNaph 2:1	14:29	4Ezra 1:13
49:25	2En 28:4 ftnt g	15:2	3En 42:2
49:27	TBenj 11:1	15:4-7	ApEl 1:4 ftnt r
49:28	ApAdam 4:9	15:6	3En 48A:1
50:6	TJac 6:3	15:7	ApEl 1:4 ftnt p
50:19-21	TJos 17:5	15:7 (LXX)	3Bar 4:3 (Slav.) ftnt e
50:25	TJos 20:2	15:11	3En 14:1 ftnt a
		15:20	3En 45:4
Exodus		15:20	2Bar 59:1
1:8-22	SibOr 11.308	15:22-25	4Ezra 1:23

Exodus (cont.)

15:26	3En 48D:10
16:1f.	SibOr 7.149
16:4	SibOr Frag 3.49
16:13	4Ezra 1:15
17:9	2Bar 59:1
17:9	3En 45:4
17:11	SibOr 8.251
17:16	3En 42:7
17:16	3En 24:20
17:19	3En 45:4
19:1f.	SibOr 3.256
19:1f.	SibOr 11.37
19:3	3En 15B:2
19:4	3En 24:11
19:9	3En 24:4
19:9	4Ezra 9:29
19:16-18	4Ezra 3:18
20:3	TAb 8:7 ftnt c
20:4	1En 68:5 ftnt l
20:11	TJob 2:4 ftnt c
21:28	2En 58:4 ftnt e
21:32	TGad 2:3 ftnt a
22:5	SibOr 2.100
22:5	SibOr 3.240
22:29	2En 2:2 ftnt g
23:21	3En 12:5
23:20-22	3En 10:5
24:5	3En 4:10 ftnt t
24:9f.	3En 1:3
24:10	3En 24:10
24:10	4Ezra 9:29
24:12	TLevi 5:4 ftnt c
24:12-18	2Bar 59:3
24:18	4Ezra 14:24
24:18	QuesEzra 38
24:18	2Bar 76:5
25:9	2Bar 4:2
25:9	2Bar 4:5
25:9	TLevi 3:5 ftnt d
25:17	2Bar 6:7
25:18-20	TSol 18:34
25:40	SibOr 4.10
25:40	2Bar 4:2
25:40	2Bar 4:5
25:40	2Bar 59:4
25:40	TLevi 3:5 ftnt d
26:30	2Bar 59:4

26:30	TLevi 3:5 ftnt d
26:31	2Bar 6:7
26:31	3En 45:1 ftnt a
27:8	TLevi 3:5 ftnt d
28:1	3En 1:3
28:3-43	TLevi 8:2
28:21	2Bar 6:7 ftnt f
28:41-43	TLevi 8:4 ftnt c
29:1-8	TLevi 8:4 ftnt c
29:5	2Bar 6:7
30:5	2Bar 42:4 ftnt d
31:2	3En 13:1 ftnt c
32:11	4Ezra 7:106
32:13	TMos 3:9
32:15f.	TLevi 5:4 ftnt c
32:29	2En 37:2
32:32f.	ApZeph 3:8 ftnt g
33:2	1En 1:9 ftnt u
33:11	2En 24:1
33:11	QuesEzra 39
33:20	SibOr 3.17
33:23	GkApEzra 6:11
34:6f.	GkApEzra 1:10 ftnt m
34:19	2En 2:2 ftnt g
34:28	3En 48D:3
34:28	4Ezra 14:24
34:28	2Bar 76:5
34:29	ApZeph 5:4 ftnt a
34:29	3En 22:7 ftnt j
34:29	3En 22:7 ftnt k
34:29f.	3En 15B:5
34:33-35	ApZeph 5:4 ftnt a
39:28	ApAb 11:3 ftnt b

Leviticus

1:1	3En 24:8
11:6	TAsh 2:9
16:1-34	TLevi 8:4 ftnt c
16:8	3En 1:1 ftnt b
16:29-31	ApEl 1:13 ftnt q2
17:10	SibOr 8.403
18:21	TSol 26:1f.
19:11	2En 42:12
19:13	TJob 12:4
19:31	SibOr 3.218f.
20:2-5	TSol 26:1f.
20:6	SibOr 3.218f.

| 20:27 | SibOr 3.218f. |
| 23:27-32 | ApEl 1:13 ftnt q2 |

Numbers

5:14	3En 23:5
7:89	3En 24:9
11:31	3En 23:4
12:8 (LXX)	GkApEzra 6:6
12:8	QuesEzra 39
13:6	2Bar 59:1
14:22	TJos 2:7 ftnt b
15:19	3En 2:3 ftnt e
20:11	4Ezra 1:20
21:14	TJob 40:14 ftnt l
23:19	2En 33:4
23:19	TJos 2:5
24:1f.	TBenj 9:2 ftnt b
24:3f.	1En 1:2
24:3f.	1En 1:3
24:17	TJud 24:1 ftnt a
24:17	TReu 6:8 ftnt c
24:17	TLevi 18:3 ftnt b
26:59	3En 45:3
29:7	ApEl 1:13 ftnt q2
30:2	2En 62:1 ftnt a
36:8	TJob 45:3 ftnt b

Deuteronomy

1:29f.	ApEl 2:3
3:9	1En 13:10
4:2	3Bar 1:7 (Slav.) ftnt h
4:12	4Ezra 9:29
4:19	3En 17:7
4:19	SibOr 3.227f.
4:24	3En 42:4
4:26	TMos 3:12
4:28	TNaph 3:3
4:35	TAb 8:7 ftnt c
4:35	SibOr 3.628
5:7	TAb 8:7 ftnt c
6:1	ApZeph 3:4
6:4	3En 15B:3
6:4	ApEl 1:3 ftnt h
6:4	ApEl 2:12
6:8	ApEl 1:9 ftnt e2
6:13	ApAdam 1:12
7:18	ApEl 1:3 ftnt h
7:18	ApEl 2:3

8:2	2En 45:3
8:2	ApEl 1:3 ftnt h
9:9	2Bar 76:5
9:9	TLevi 5:4 ftnt c
9:11	TLevi 5:4 ftnt c
9:15	TLevi 5:4 ftnt c
9:18	2Bar 76:5
9:26	2Bar 5:1
9:29	2Bar 5:1
10:4	3En 48D:4
10:5	2Bar 6:7
10:14-17 (LXX)	ApZeph A ftnt a
10:17	2Bar 13:9
11:2	TJob 38:1 ftnt a
13:1	3Bar 1:7 (Slav.) ftnt h
13:3	2En 30:15
14:7	TAsh 2:9
18:1f.	ApEl 1:3 ftnt h
18:10	SibOr 3.218f.
18:15	TBenj 9:2 ftnt b
19:14	SibOr 2.100
19:14	SibOr 3.240
19:15 (LXX)	TAb 13:8 ftnt d
20:1	ApEl 2:2 ftnt e
20:3	ApEl 1:3 ftnt h
22:21	TLevi 7:3
24:13 (5 sic)-15	TJob 12:2 ftnt b
25:5-10	TZeb 3:4
26:5-10	ApEl 1:3 ftnt k
26:8	ApEl 5:1
26:15	TMos 10:3
28:12	1En 11:1
28:23	SibOr 3.539
28:30-33	SibOr 3.268
28:37	SibOr 3.272
28:56	SibOr 3.527
29:2	ApEl 5:1
29:21-23	SibOr 3.273
29:25	ApEl 1:13 ftnt r2
29:25-28	SibOr 3.275
30:3	2Bar 78:7
30:15	SibOr 8.399
30:15	TAsh 1:3 ftnt a
30:15-20	TLevi 19:2
30:19	2Bar 19:1
30:19	TMos 3:12
30:19-20	2Bar 84:4 ftnt f

Deuteronomy (cont.)
31:3-8   TMos 12:8
31:7   TMos 1:6
31:14f.   TMos 1:9
31:15   3En 24:7
31:16   TMos 5:3
31:20   4Ezra 2:19
31:28   2Bar 19:1
31:28   TMos 3:12
32:2   2Bar 41:4 ftnt b
32:2   ApocEzek Frag. 1
                  ftnt k
32:11-13   TMos 10:8 ftnt e
32:12   3En 48A:10
32:13   TJob 13:2 ftnt b
32:17   2Bar 10:8 ftnt e
32:17   TSol 5:5
32:21 (LXX)   3Bar 16:3
32:30   SibOr 3.533
32:30 (LXX)   ApDan 4:14
32:35   2En 50:4
32:35   TGad 6:7
32:39   2En 33:8
32:39   2En 36:1
32:39   2En 47:3
32:41   3En 32:2
32:41   3En 32:1 ftnt c
32:43   SibOr 3.313
33:1   2En 7:4
33:1f.   TLevi 6:6 ftnt c
33:2   ApZeph 3:2
33:8-10   TReu 6:8
33:12   TBenj 11:1
33:13-17   TNaph 5:6 ftnt c
33:19-20   2Bar 84:2
33:22   ApDan 8:2 ftnt b
34:1-3   2Bar 76:3
34:5-8   TMos 1:15 ftnt j
34:7   2Bar 17:4

Joshua
1:7   TMos 1:10
3:14-16   4Ezra 13:44
5:13   3En 22:6
5:13-15 (LXX)   TAb 1:4 ftnt c
5:14 (LXX)   3Bar 1:8 (Gk.) ftnt k
5:14 (LXX)   3Bar 11:4 (Gk.) ftnt c
7:6f.   4Ezra 7:106

7:9   2Bar 5:1
10:12   2En 14:3
10:12   SibOr 5.258
10:13   TJob 40:14 ftnt l
14:10   TMos 2:3 ftnt e
18:16   TSol 26:1f.
18:28   TSol 26:1f.
23:14   2Bar 44:3
24:15   TGad 1:3 ftnt a
24:18   2Bar 60:2

Judges
3:5   2Bar 60:2
5:4   ApZeph 3:2
5:4f.   SibOr 3.675
5:20   SibOr 5.212 ftnt y2
5:24   2Bar 54:11
5:25   TJob 13:2 ftnt b
5:31   3En 48A:9 ftnt w
7:22   TLevi 2:3 ftnt b
8:19   TSol 1:13
9:53   TSol 12:3 ftnt a
13:22   SibOr 3.17
18:11-31   TDan 5:6 ftnt b

Ruth
2:12   2Bar 41:5
2:12   3En 7:1 ftnt c
4:7-8   TZeb 3:4 ftnt a
4:15   TJob 1:2 ftnt e

1 Samuel
1:1   3En 45:4
1:3   3En 45:4
1:20   3En 45:4
2:13   3En 4:10 ftnt t
2:35   2En 69:4
2:51   TJob 1:2 ftnt e
3:10   2En 1:5 ftnt p
4:4   3En 22:12
4:4   3En 22:16
7:9   4Ezra 7:106
8:1f.   ApAdam 7:49 ftnt u
12:17   3En 48A:7
12:20   2En 2:2
12:23   4Ezra 7:106
14:32-34   1En 7:4
15:29   2En 33:4

16:23	3En 23:8	8:22	2En 69:14
17:1-54	TJud 3:1 ftnt a	8:22	2En 70:16
17:4	TJud 3:7	8:22f.	4Ezra 7:109
17:10	3En 15B:2	8:30	4Ezra 7:109
21:5	2En 71:2 ftnt d	8:54	2En 69:14
		8:54	2En 70:16
2 Samuel		8:62-63	2Bar 61:3
1:18	TJob 25:1 ftnt a	8:66	2En 69:19
1:18	TJob 40:14 ftnt l	9:15	SibOr 11.80 ftnt s
1:19	TJob 25:1 ftnt a	9:15	SibOr 11.90
1:25	TJob 25:1 ftnt a	10:1-10	TSol 19:2
1:27	TJob 25:1 ftnt a	10:1-10	TSol 21:1
3:31-34	ApZeph 1:2 ftnt b	10:1-13	TSol 19:3
5:6f.	TSol 26:1f.	11:1-8	TSol 26:1
7:16	SibOr 7.32	11:1-8	TSol 26:6
17:10	3En 15B:2	11:5	TSol 8:10
17:29	TJob 13:2 ftnt b	11:7	TSol 26:1f.
21:19-22	TJud 3:7	11:33	TSol 26:1f.
22:11	3En 23:16	11:41	TJob 40:14 ftnt l
22:11	3En 24:1	12:1f.	TSol 5:5
22:11	GkApEzra 7:5	12:1f.	TSol 15:8
22:16	1En 18:2	12:1f.	TSol 15:12
24:17	4Ezra 7:109	12:21	TJos 19:2 ftnt a
		12:32	2Bar 62:2
1 Kings		14:19	TJob 40:14 ftnt l
1:1-4	TSol 26:2 ftnt a	14:29	TJob 40:14 ftnt l
1:15	TSol 26:2 ftnt a	15:7	TJob 40:14 ftnt l
2:2	2Bar 44:3	17:6	2Bar 77:25
2:13-25	TSol 26:2 ftnt a	17:20f.	4Ezra 7:109
2:13-46	TSol 26:1f.	18:4	2Bar 62:3
2:17-22	TSol 26:2 ftnt a	18:42	4Ezra 7:109
2:25	TSol 8:9 ftnt j	18:45	4Ezra 7:109
3:12	2Bar 61:5	19:4	2Bar 3:7
3:12	TLevi 2:3 ftnt b	19:11	3En 23:6
3:13	2En 69:5	19:11	3En 23:12
4:29-34 (LXX)	TSol 3:5	19:12	3En 22C:5 ftnt m
4:29-34	TSol 4:11	22:19	1En 14:18
4:29-34	TSol 22:1	22:19	2En 20:1
4:29-34	TSol 23:4	22:19	3En 5:8
5:1f.	TSol 19:2	22:19	3En 18:24
5:1–ch. 8	SibOr 11.87	22:19	ApZeph A
6:1–ch. 7	TSol 1:1		
6:23-28	TSol 18:34	*2 Kings*	
7:2	TSol 8:12	1:2	TSol 3:1 ftnt a
7:2f.	TSol 23:3	1:6	TSol 3:1 ftnt a
7:23f.	TSol 21:4	1:15	2En 1:7
7:48-50	TSol 21:2	2:3	2En 1a:1 ftnt d
8:1f.	2Bar 61:2	2:9 (LXX)	TJob 39:12 ftnt e

2 Kings (cont.)

2:10-12	TJob 52:9 ftnt j
2:11	3En 6:1
2:11	ApZeph 5:4 ftnt a
2:11	ApDan 14:2 ftnt b
2:11	TJob 52:6 ftnt e
2:11f.	4Ezra 6:26
2:11f.	GkApEzra 7:5
2:11f.	QuesEzra 40
4:38-41	TJos 6:2 ftnt a
5:10	3En 36:2
5:14	3En 36:2
6:17	TJob 52:9 ftnt j
6:28-29	2Bar 62:5
11:18	3En 45:2 ftnt i
16:3	TMos 2:8
16:20	2Bar 63:2
17:1-6	4Ezra 13:40
17:3-6	2Bar 62:7
17:21-23	2Bar 1:1f.
18:13-37	2Bar 63:2
19:14-19	2Bar 63:5
19:15-19	4Ezra 7:110
19:35	TAdam 4:7
19:35-36	2Bar 63:7 ftnt a
21:2	2Bar 64:2
21:6	TMos 2:8
22:1	2Bar 66:1f.
22:16	2Bar 1:1f.
22:20	1En 81:9
23:4-30	2Bar 66:1f.
23:10	SibOr 2.292 ftnt x2
23:10	3En 44:3
23:10	TSol 26:1f.
23:11	TSol 6:10
23:24f.	SibOr 3.227f.
23:27	2Bar 1:1f.
24:3	2Bar 1:1f.
24:8	2Bar 1:1
24:9	2Bar 1:1
24:12	2Bar 1:1
25:1f.	4Ezra 3:1
25:3-4	2Bar 8:1
25:7	2Bar 8:5
25:8-17	TSol 15:8
25:11	2Bar 8:5
25:13	TSol 21:4

1 Chronicles

1:1	2En 33:10
1:1-16	ApAdam 4:9
1:1f.	2En 71:32 ftnt o
6:4-8	ApZeph 3:4 ftnt c
6:50-53	ApZeph 3:4 ftnt c
11:4f.	TSol 26:1f.
18:17 (LXX)	TMos 1:6 ftnt d
18:18	TSol 21:4
29:29	TJob 40:14 ftnt l
38:9	2En 66:3

2 Chronicles

3:14	3En 45:1 ftnt a
4:2	TSol 21:4
6:30	2En 66:3
9:1-10	TSol 19:2
9:1-10	TSol 21:1
9:1-12	TSol 19:3
9:29	TJob 40:14 ftnt l
12:3 (LXX)	TZeb 4:6 ftnt b
12:15	TJob 40:14 ftnt l
18:18	3En 18:24
20:7	TAb 1:6 ftnt g
20:34	TJob 40:14 ftnt l
26:11 (LXX)	TMos 1:6 ftnt d
26:16-21	TJob 32:8 ftnt l
26:22	TJob 40:14 ftnt l
28:7 (LXX)	TMos 1:6 ftnt d
32:21	2Bar 63:7 ftnt a
32:31	2En 45:3
33:3	1En 48:3 ftnt d
33:3	1En 72:12 ftnt y
33:7	2Bar 64:3 ftnt a
33:10-13	2Bar 64:8 ftnt c
33:18f.	TJob 40:14 ftnt l
34:28	2Bar 1:1f.
35:25	TJob 40:14 ftnt l
35:35	TJob 25:1 ftnt a
36:7	TMos 3:2
36:9 (LXX)	2Bar 1:1
36:22-23	TMos 4:6

Ezra

1:1-4	TMos 4:6
1:2-7	TJob 17:2 ftnt a
1:7-11	SibOr 3.291
1:26-28	ApZeph A

3:2	4Ezra 3:1 ftnt a	1:6	3En 26:12
3:12	2Bar 68:6	1:14-19	TJob 16:1 ftnt a
5:1f.	SibOr 3.290	1:18	TJob 15:3
5:2	4Ezra 3:1 ftnt a	1:18-21 (LXX)	TJob 19:2 ftnt b
6:6-12	TMos 4:7	1:18f.	TJob 1:2 ftnt e
7:2-5	ApZeph 3:4 ftnt c	1:18f.	TJob 18:1 ftnt a
7:11	SibOr 11.80 ftnt s	1:19	3En 23:14
7:12	TMos 8:1	1:19	TJob 18:1
7:14-23	SibOr 3.291	1:20	TJob 23:7 ftnt e
10:6	ApEl 1:13 ftnt q2	1:21	SibOr 8.96f.
10:10	TJob 45:3 ftnt b	1:21	2En 1a:1 ftnt d
		1:21b	TJob 19:4
Nehemiah		1:22	TJob 16:7
1:4	ApEl 1:13 ftnt q2	2:7f.	TJob 20:6
1:10	ApEl 1:4 ftnt p	2:8	TJob 21:1
2:17	TMos 4:7	2:8 (LXX)	TJob 20:7 ftnt e
6:15-16	TMos 4:7	2:8b-9d	TJob 24:1
9:6	TJob 2:4 ftnt c	2:8b-9e (LXX)	TJob 24:2 ftnt c
9:12	TSol 23:2	2:9	TJob 24:2 ftnt c
9:19	TSol 23:2	2:9	TJob 43:5 ftnt f
12:1	4Ezra 3:1 ftnt a	2:9 (LXX)	TJob 20:8 ftnt f
12:4	2Bar 5:5	2:9 (LXX)	TJob 21:1 ftnt a
12:43	3En 48A:3	2:9e	TJob 25:10
14:3	4Ezra 1:18	2:9e (LXX[A])	TJob 25:10 ftnt e
		2:9e	TJob 26:2
Esther		2:10	TJob 16:7
6:1	3En 27:2	2:10	TJob 20:9 ftnt g
8:9	SibOr 11.65 ftnt p	2:10	TJob 26:4
8:9	SibOr 11.69 ftnt q	2:10	TJob 26:6
		2:11	TJob 29:3
Job		2:11 (LXX)	TJob 3:7 ftnt d
1:1	TJob 44:3 ftnt b	2:11-13	TJob 28:2
1:1	TJob 25:1 ftnt b	2:13 (LXX)	TJob 28:3 ftnt d
1:1-4 (LXX)	TJob 15:1 ftnt a	3:11	4Ezra 5:35
1:2	TJob 1:3	4:8	2En 42:11
1:2	TJob 17:5	5:8 (LXX)	TJob 38:1 ftnt b
1:3	TJob 1:2 ftnt e	5:22	TJob 32:11
1:3	TJob 9:2	7:2	TJob 12:3
1:3	TJob 9:4	7:2	TJob 12:4 ftnt b
1:3	TJob 9:6	7:5	TJob 20:7
1:3	TJob 10:5	7:7	2Bar 14:10
1:3	TJob 28:6	7:12	4Ezra 6:50
1:3	TJob 32:3 ftnt e	9:2	1En 81:5
1:4	TJob 15:3	9:9	TSol 8:2 ftnt a
1:5	TJob 15:4	9:32	TJob 43:13
1:6	3En 4:6	10:18-19	4Ez 5:35
1:6	3En 5:10	11:13	2Bar 32:1
1:6	3En 14:1	12:4	TJob 32:11

Job (cont.)

12:4 (LXX)	TJob 32:11 ftnt n
12:25	TJob 43:6 ftnt g
14:1	3En 6:2
14:11	TJob 33:6
15:14	3En 2:2
15:14	3En 6:2
16:3	TJob 9:2
16:3	TJob 9:4
16:3	TJob 10:5
16:14 (LXX)	TJob 29:4 ftnt b
17:6	TJob 32:11 ftnt n
17:12	TJob 43:6 ftnt g
17:15 (LXX)	TJob 37:1 ftnt a
17:20	TJob 13:2 ftnt b
18:5	TJob 43:5
18:5f.	TJob 43:6 ftnt g
18:6	TJob 43:6 ftnt g
18:17	TJob 43:6 ftnt g
18:17 (LXX)	TJob 43:5 ftnt f
18:18	TJob 43:6 ftnt g
19:9	TJob 3:7 ftnt d
20:14	TJob 43:12
20:16	TJob 43:8
21:12	TJob 14:2-3
21:14	3En 4:3
21:17	TJob 43:6 ftnt g
22:9 (LXX)	TJob 10:2 ftnt b
23:11	TJob 43:6 ftnt g
25:2	3En 42:7
25:4	3En 2:2
25:5	2En 11:2 ftnt g
26:4	TJob 43:2 ftnt a
26:10	2En 28:4
26:10	TJob 43:6 ftnt g
26:11	1En 18:4
26:12f.	4Ezra 6:50
29:1f. (LXX)	TJob 9:1 ftnt a
29:1–ch. 31	TJob 11:1 ftnt a
29:3	TJob 43:6 ftnt g
29:5	TJob 32:6
29:6	TJob 13:1
29:7	TJob 32:8 ftnt l
29:7-25	TJob 32:8 ftnt l
29:13b (LXX)	TJob 10:2 ftnt b
29:15 (LXX)	TJob 53:2 ftnt c
29:15f.	TJob 53:2
30:1	TJob 9:3
30:1	TJob 32:11 ftnt n
30:9	TJob 32:11 ftnt n
30:19	TJob 38:2
31:1f.	ApZeph 7:4
31:1f. (LXX)	TJob 9:1 ftnt a
31:6	4Ezra 3:34
31:16b (LXX)	TJob 10:2 ftnt b
31:24	TJob 28:5
31:30	TJob 32:11 ftnt n
31:31	TJob 13:6
31:31 (LXX)	TJob 13:4 ftnt c
31:32	TJob 9:7
31:32	1En 72:5 ftnt n
31:34	TJob 10:4
31:36f.	TJob 11:11
31:37	TJob 11:12 ftnt d
31:39 (LXX)	TJob 12:4 ftnt b
32:2	TJob 9:2
32:2	TJob 9:4
32:2	TJob 25:1 ftnt b
32:2-12	TJob 25:1 ftnt a
32:3	TJob 10:5
32:8	TJob 41:5 ftnt c
32:18-20	TJob 41:5 ftnt c
36:2	TJob 41:3
36:27	2En 47:5
36:28b	TJob 35:4
36:28b	TJob 38:7
36:29	1En 18:5
37:16	1En 18:5
37:14	2En 54:1
37:16	2En 54:1
38:1	TJob 42:1
38:1	TJob 42:2 ftnt a
38:1 (LXX)	TJob 47:9 ftnt g
38:1f.	2En 24:2 ftnt c
38:1–ch. 41	SibOr 8.361f.
38:1–ch. 42	SibOr Frag 3.15
38:3	TJob 44:1 ftnt a
38:3	TJob 46:7 ftnt d
38:3	TJob 47:5
38:3	TJob 46:8 ftnt e
38:6	1En 18:2
38:7	3En 38:3
38:7	ApEl 4:11
38:8-11	SibOr 1.321
38:10	2En 28:4 ftnt g
38:11	2En 28:4

38:22	2En 5:1	11:5f.	TZeb 10:2
38:22	2En 40:10	11:5f.	TZeb 10:3 ftnt b
38:22	3En 22B:4	11:6	SibOr 3.690
40:2	TJob 47:5	11:6	ApAdam 5:10
40:7	TJob 46:7 ftnt d	14:1	1En 81:5
40:7	TJob 46:8 ftnt e	14:1	4Ezra 8:58
40:7 (RSV)	TJob 44:1 ftnt a	14:2	3En 24:17
40:15	3En 48D:8	16 (LXX 15):10	ApZeph 5:5 ftnt a
41:4	3En 48D:8	17 (LXX 16):15	2En 22:6 ftnt k
42:4	TJob 46:8 ftnt e	18:1f.	TSol 18:34
42:4 (RSV)	TJob 46:7 ftnt d	18:2	3En 22B:6 ftnt g
42:7-9	TJob 42:4 ftnt e	18:5	SibOr 2.240 ftnt t2
42:7-10	TJob 42:4f.	18:7	SibOr 3.675
42:8	TJob 15:1 ftnt a	18:10	1En 14:8
42:10-12	TJob 44:4 ftnt c	18:10	3En 22:11
42:10f.	TJob 44:3	18:10	3En 23:16
42:11	TJob 44:5 ftnt d	18:10	3En 24:1
42:14	TJob 1:4	18:10	3En 24:2
42:15	TJob 46:4	18:10	3En 24:17
42:15b	TJob 46:4 ftnt c	18:11	1En 14:8
42:16	TJob 16:1 ftnt c	18:11	GkApEzra 7:5
42:16 (LXX)	TJob 53:8 ftnt f	18:15	1En 18:2
42:17a	TJob 4:10	18:15	4Ezra 16:12
42:17a (LXX)	TJob 39:12 ftnt e	19:1	3En 46: (13 sic)3
42:17a (LXX)	TJob 53:8 ftnt f	19:1	SibOr 5.428
42:17b, e (LXX[A])	TJob 25:1 ftnt b	19:8 (ET 7)	3En 11:1 ftnt b
42:17b, e (LXX[A])	TJob 44:3 ftnt b	19:10	1En 82:4
42:17c	TJob 1:6	20:6	3En 44:7
		22:1	TSol 6:8
Psalms		22:6	2En 45:3
1:1f.	TLevi 13:1 ftnt a	24:2	2En 28:4
1:3	ApAdam 6:2	24:4	ApEl 1:20
1:6	SibOr 8.399 ftnt p2	24 (23):7	1En 72:5 ftnt n
2:1f.	SibOr 3.663	24 (Slav. 23):7	2En 16:1 ftnt b
2:7	2En 67:1 ftnt a	24:7-10	TLevi 5:1 ftnt a
2:7	TLevi 4:2 ftnt a	24 (23):8	1En 72:5 ftnt n
2:9	SibOr 8.248	24 (Slav. 23):9	2En 16:1 ftnt b
2:11	ApAdam 1:12	24:12 (LXX)	3Bar 2:1 (Gk.) ftnt c
5:8	TSim 5:2 ftnt a	28:3	2En 52:14
7:10	2Bar 48:39	28:9	4Ezra 8:16
7:16	2En 60:3-4	29:1	3En 14:1 ftnt a
8:3	3En 46: (14 sic)4	29 (LXX 28):3	ApEl 1:5 ftnt t
8:4	3En 5:10	29:5	2Bar 36:6
8:5-8	SibOr Frag 3.13	29:7	3En 6:2 ftnt g
8:6-8	4Ezra 6:46	33:6	SibOr 1.19
9:15	2En 60:3-4	33:6	SibOr 3.20
10:1	3En 44:10	33:6	2Bar 14:17
10:18	2En 42:9	33:6	2Bar 21:4

Psalms (cont.)

33:6	TAb 9:6 ftnt b
33:9	2En 33:4
33:9	ApAb 22:2
35:8	2En 60:3-4
36:8	2Bar 41:5
40:6	2En 45:3
40:6	2Bar 54:13
40:6 (LXX)	3Bar 2:1 (Gk.) ftnt c
40:7	ApZeph 3:8 ftnt g
42:3	3Bar 1:2
42:10	3Bar 1:2
44:22	4Ezra 15:10
45:1f.	TJud 24:3
45:2	3En 48D:4 ftnt j
45:4 (LXX)	TJud 24:1 ftnt a
46:9	SibOr 5.381
47:5	3En 5:14
47:5	3En 24:12
47:5	3En 48C:1
47:8	3En 24:19
50:4	ApocEzek Frag 1 (Bavli, Sanhedrin 91a, b) and ftnt k
50:21 (LXX)	ApDan 14:12
51:10	2En 45:3
51:16	2En 45:3
51:19	ApDan 14:12
53:1	4Ezra 8:58
53:9	TJud 24:1 ftnt a
55:17	2En 51:4
55:21	2En 52:14
57:2	2Bar 41:5
57:6	2En 60:3-4
60:3	SibOr Frag 3.39
62:4	2En 52:14
62:9	4Ezra 3:34
63 (LXX 62):3	2En 22:6 ftnt k
65:7	SibOr 1.314
65:7	SibOr 1.321
66 (LXX 65):10-12	TAb 12:14 ftnt g
68:4	3En 19:7
68:4	3En 24:13
68:7f.	4Ezra 3:18
68:12	3En 17:8 ftnt r
68:17	3En 24:6
68:18 (ET 17)	3En 7:1 ftnt g
69:2f.	SibOr 2.240 ftnt t2
69:21	SibOr 6.24
69:21	SibOr 8.303
69:21	GkApEzra 2:25
69:21	GkApEzra 7:1
69:28	ApZeph 3:8 ftnt g
70 (71):19	TJob 38:1 ftnt a
71:17	2En 54:1
71 (72):20	TJob 49:3 ftnt b
72:11	2Bar 72:3 ftnt b
72:17	2Bar 72:3 ftnt b
72:18	TSol 1:0
74:12-15	4Ezra 6:50
74:12-17	TAsh 7:3 ftnt a
74:19	4Ezra 5:26
75:7	2En 8:4 ftnt k
75:9	2Bar 13:8
77:18	3En 38:2
78:5f.	1En 82:2
78:23	3Bar 2:2 ftnt e
78:25	4Ezra 1:19
78:25	2Bar 29:8
78:54	3En 48A:1
79:10	3Bar 1:2
79:13	4Ezra 5:26
80:1	SibOr 3.2
80:8	4Ezra 5:23
80:8-16	3Bar 1:2
80:13	4Ezra 15:30
82:1	3En 15B:1
85:10	1En 11:2
86:16	GkApEzra 1:10 ftnt m
89:7	3En 4:1 ftnt a
89:1-4	TJud 22:3
89:14	3En 31:1
89 (LXX 88):22	ApEl 1:10 ftnt g2
89:34-37	TJud 22:3
89:36	SibOr 7.32
90:4	ApEl 5:37 ftnt p3
90:9-10	2Bar 16:1
91:1f.	ApZeph 1:2 ftnt b
92:5	3En 47:4
93:1	SibOr 1.9
93:1f.	SibOr 8.431
94:9	SibOr 8.369
94:11	2En 53:3
94:11	2En 66:3
95:6	SibOr 3.716

95:11	ApEl 2:53 ftnt t3	115:16	2En 22:6 ftnt j
97:1f.	SibOr 8.431	118:22	TSol 22:7
97:2	3En 22:15	118:22	TSol 23:4
97:2	SibOr 1.10	119:4	ApZeph 3:4
97:3	3En 40:3	119:37	2En 9:1
97:3	SibOr 3.761	119:75	ApEl 5:24 ftnt u2
99:1	SibOr 3.2	119:89	3En 28:4 ftnt c
99:6	3En 48A:7	119:92-93	2Bar 46:3
99:7	TSol 23:3	119:103	1En 82:4
101:5	2En 60:5	119:105	2Bar 17:4
104:2	1En 14:18	120:3	2En 63:4 ftnt e
104:2	2En 47:4	120:7	2En 52:13
104:3	1En 14:8	122:1	SibOr 3.718
104:3	3En 24:14	132:11	SibOr 7.32
104:4	1En 17:1	132:13	4Ezra 5:26
104:4	2En 29:1	135:13	2Bar 5:2
104:4	2En 39:5 ftnt d	136 (135):25	GkApEzra 7:9
104:4	3En 22:4 ftnt e	139:8-12	2En 66:4
104:4	4Ezra 8:22	139:12	ApZeph 2:6f.
104:4	2Bar 21:6	139:14	2En 54:1
104:4	TAdam 1:12	139:14f.	4Ezra 8:15
104:9	2En 28:4	139:23	2En 45:3
104:9	SibOr 1.321	144:15	3En 2:4
104:13	3En 42:2	145 (146):6	TJob 2:4 ftnt c
104:21 (LXX)	2En 58:3	146:4	2Bar 14:10
104:24	3En 45:6	147:4	3En 46:2
104:29	2En 33:4 ftnt f	147:8	2En 30:1
105:14	VisEzra 7	148:1f.	SibOr 8.431
105:14	VisEzra 17	148:1f.	TAdam 2:2
105 (106):21	TJob 38:1 ftnt a	148:7	TAsh 7:3 ftnt a
106:34-39	TMos 2:9	148:7f.	TAdam 1:3
106:37	TSol 5:5	148:8	3En 23:15
106:37	2Bar 10:8 ftnt e	148:8	2En 5:1 ftnt c
107:16	ApZeph 5:6	150:6	2En 51:5
107 (106):16	1En 72:5 ftnt n		
107:22	2Bar 54:11	*Proverbs*	
109 (110):1	TJob 33:3 ftnt g	1:1	TSol 3:5
110:1f.	TLevi 4:2 ftnt a	1:1	TSol 22:1
110:1f.	TLevi 18:2 ftnt a	3:18	2En 8:2
110:1f.	TReu 6:11 ftnt e	3:11-12	2Bar 13:10
110:3	2En 12:2	4:10-14	SibOr 8.399 ftnt p2
110:4	TLevi 8:4 ftnt a	4:11	2En 42:10
114:4	1En 51:4	4:11	2Bar 38:3
115:2	3Bar 1:2	6:16-17	2En 63:4
115:5-7	ApAb (superscrip-	6:23-35	TSim 5:2 ftnt a
	tion) ftnt a	6:29	2En 59:1 ftnt a
115:5-7	ApAb 7:1f. ftnt a	7:1-17	TSim 5:2 ftnt a
115:13	ApEl 5:4 ftnt m	8:1f.	2En 24:2 ftnt c

Proverbs (cont.)

8:22-26	2En 26:2 ftnt b
8:27 (LXX)	2En 25:4
8:29	2En 28:4
8:29	SibOr 1.321
8:30	2En 30:8
8:35	TSim 5:2 ftnt a
11:8	3En 48C:11
11:30	2En 8:2
11:31 (LXX)	ApDan 11:11
13:12	2En 8:2
13:14	2Bar 46:3
14:31	2En 44:2
15:4	2En 8:2
15:8	ApSedr 1:8
15:11	2En 66:3
16:2	4Ezra 3:34
16:22	2Bar 38:1
19:17	2En 50:5
20:22	2En 50:4
22:2	2En 8:2
22:8	2En 42:11
22:8	TLevi 13:6
22:8 (LXX)	TJob 12:1 ftnt a
22:14	2En 8:2
23:32	TAb 17:14 ftnt b
24:29	2En 50:4
25:21	TJob 7:11
25:23	3En 23:10
26:27	2En 60:3-4
27:20	2Bar 56:6
28:10	2En 60:3-4
31:20	2En 51:1
31:26	2En 42:12

Ecclesiastes

1:1	TSol 3:5
1:1	TSol 22:1
1:6	3En 23:17
2:1-8	SibOr 12.289
3:5	TNaph 8:8
3:16	ApZeph 3:1
5:14	SibOr 8.96f.
7:17	TJob 20:8 ftnt f
8:4f.	3En 45:6
9:5	2Bar 11:6
11:30	TJob 27:1 ftnt b
12:7	ApEl 4:25

Song of Solomon

1:1	TSol 3:5
1:1	TSol 22:1
2:1	TSim 6:2 ftnt a
2:2	4Ezra 5:24
4:8	1En 13:10
4:16	3En 23:18
6:3	TSol 26:1f.
6:12	TSol 26:2 ftnt a
7:1	TSol 26:2 ftnt a

Isaiah

1:2	ApEl 5:25 ftnt v2
1:8	TJos 19:12 ftnt d
1:11	2En 45:3
1:11	SibOr 8.390
1:15	4Ezra 1:26
1:16	SibOr 4.165
1:17	2En 9:1
1:17	2En 42:9
1:18	ApocEzek Frag 2
2:3	SibOr 3.718
2:3	SibOr 3.772
2:4	SibOr 5.381
2:4	ApDan 5:11
2:12	SibOr 3.741
2:18	SibOr 8.224
2:18-20	SibOr 3.608
5:1f.	3Bar 1:2
5:2	TJos 19:12 ftnt d
5:14	2Bar 56:6
5:10	1En 10:19
5:16	3En 24:21
5:20	3Bar 4:15 (Gk.) ftnt x
5:23	TMos 5:5
5:24	ApEl 1:4 ftnt p
6:1	2En 20:3
6:1	3En 24:23
6:1f.	1En 14:18
6:1f.	2En 20:1
6:1f.	TLevi 2:5 ftnt c
6:1f.	TLevi 3:4 ftnt c
6:1-2	2Bar 21:7
6:1-3	QuesEzra 29
6:1-5	TLevi 5:1
6:1-8	ApZeph A
6:2	3En 22:13

6:2	3En 26:8	11:15f.	4Ezra 13:47
6:2	ApEl 5:2	12:6	SibOr 3.785
6:2f.	TSol 18:34	13:1f.	SibOr 5.434f.
6:2f.	TAdam 1:4	13:9-13	TLevi 3:9 ftnt e
6:2-3	2En 21:1	13:10	ApAdam 5:10
6:3	3En 1:3	13:21	2Bar 10:8
6:3	3En 19:7	13:22	2Bar 10:8 ftnt f
6:3	3En 20:2	13:47	SibOr 3.302
6:3	3En 35:6	14:1f.	2En 29:3 ftnt i
6:3	3En 40:2	14:3	SibOr 5.173
6:3	3En 22B:7	14:12	2Bar 4:7 (Slav.) ftnt o
6:3	3En 48B:2	14:12	ApEl 4:11 ftnt u
6:3f.	3En 38:1	14:12	SibOr 5.72
6:3	TAb 20:12 ftnt i	14:12	SibOr 5.212 ftnt y2
6:4	TLevi 3:10	14:12 (LXX)	GkApEzra 4:28
6:6f.	3En 36:2 ftnt d	14:12	ApEl 4:11
6:9f.	SibOr 1.360f.	14:13	SibOr 1.314
7:12-14	SibOr 5.157 ftnt n2	14:13-15	GkApEzra 4:32
7:14	ApocEzek Frag 3	14:13-16	SibOr 3.360
7:14	TSol 6:8	14:14	2En 29:4
7:14	TSol 11:6	14:15	SibOr 5.177
7:14	TSol 15:12	14:15	SibOr 8.100
7:15	TJob 13:2 ftnt b	16:5	3En 31:2
8:8	TSol 6:8	17:6	4Ezra 16:29
8:8	TSol 11:6	17:12	SibOr 1.314
8:8	TSol 15:12	19:1f.	SibOr 3.313
8:14f.	SibOr 1.346	19:1	3En 24:3
8:19	2Bar 14:5	19:1	3En 24:17
8:19f.	SibOr 3.227f.	19:1	GkApEzra 5:7 ftnt b
9:2	2En 46:3	19:2	4Ezra 13:31
9:5	3En 26:8	19:5-8	SibOr 5.92 ftnt x
9:6	TSol 12:3	19:19	SibOr 5.501
9:6	ApEl 2:6 ftnt p	21:9	2Bar 70:10
11:1	SibOr 6.8	21:11	ApZeph 3:2
11:1	SibOr 6.16	24:17-20	TLevi 3:9 ftnt e
11:1	SibOr 7.38	24:18-23	TLevi 3:10
11:1	SibOr 8.254	24:19f.	3En 48A:4
11:1	TJud 24:4 ftnt c	24:22-23	TLevi 18:12 ftnt e
11:1-3	TLevi 2:3 ftnt b	25:8	ApEl 5:38 ftnt r3
11:2	3En 23:9	26:4	3En 42:5
11:2	TLevi 18:7	26:19 (LXX)	ApocEzek Frag 1,
11:2	TJud 24:2 ftnt b		Introduction
11:4	4Ezra 13:10	26:19	2Bar 29:8
11:4	2Bar 40:2 ftnt a	26:20	1En 72:5 ftnt n
11:6	SibOr 13.28	26:21	1En 1:4
11:6-8	SibOr 3.788	27:1	3En 32:1 ftnt c
11:6-9	2Bar 73:7	27:1	SibOr 8.88 ftnt m
11:9	TLevi 18:5	27:1	2Bar 29:4

Isaiah (cont.)

27:1	TAsh 7:3 ftnt a
27:13	GkApEzra 4:36 ftnt n
28:5	GkApEzra 6:17 ftnt f
28:9	3En 48C:12
28:16	TSol 22:7
29:6	SibOr 3.690
30:1	ApEl 1:2
30:7	4Ezra 6:50
30:17	SibOr 3.533
30:25	SibOr 3.682
30:26	2En 11:1 ftnt d
30:26	2En 66:8 ftnt d
30:26	3En 26:5
30:30	1En 14:11
30:30	SibOr 3.690
31:7	SibOr 3.605
31:21	TSol 7:7 ftnt e
32:17	1En 11:2
33:3	3En 18:7
33:7	3En 33:1 ftnt a
33:15	2En 9:1
34:1b	ApZeph 3:8 ftnt g
34:4	SibOr 3.82
34:4	SibOr 8.233
34:4	SibOr 8.413
34:5	3En 32:1 ftnt c
34:11f.	TSol 7:7 ftnt e
34:11-15	SibOr 8.41
34:13	2Bar 10:8
34:14	2Bar 10:8
35:1	TSim 6:2 ftnt a
37:36	TAdam 4:7
40:4	SibOr 3.680
40:4	SibOr 8.234
40:6-7	2Bar 82:7
40:11 (LXX)	GkApEzra 7:6 ftnt a
40:12	2En 47:6
40:12 (LXX)	GkApEzra 7:5
40:13	2En 33:4
40:13f.	2Bar 75:2
40:15	ApZeph 2:5
40:15	4Ezra 6:57
40:15	2Bar 82:5
40:15 (LXX)	2Bar 82:6 ftnt i
40:18-26	SibOr 3.12f.
40:19f.	SibOr 5.80
40:21-26	ApEl 1:3 ftnt j

40:22	2En 47:4
40:22	3En 17:6
40:26	3En 46:2
40:28-31	TJos 2:5
40:28-31	TJud 25:5
40:31	TMos 10:8 ftnt e
41:8	ApAb 9:7
41:8 (LXX)	TAb 1:6 ftnt g
41:10	SibOr 3.709
41:17-20	ApEl 1:3 ftnt j
42:1	2Bar 70:10
42:1	TBenj 11:2
42:1	ApAdam 6:9 ftnt f
42:2	2Bar 72:3 ftnt b
42:5	2En 47:4
42:5	3En 44:7
42:6	ApAdam 6:1 ftnt b
42:9	2Bar 70:10
43:10	2Bar 70:10
43:11	SibOr 3.628
43:11	SibOr 5.173 ftnt q2
43:20	2Bar 10:8
44:6	2En 33:8
44:6	2En 36:1
44:6	2En 47:3
44:6	SibOr 5.173 ftnt q2
44:6	SibOr 8.377
44:6	4Ezra 8:7
44:6	TIsaac 6:34
44:8-20	SibOr 3.586
44:9-20	SibOr 5.80
44:9-20	SibOr 8.378
44:21	2Bar 70:10
44:23	TLevi 18:5
44:24	2En 47:4
44:24f.	ApEl 1:3 ftnt j
44:25	SibOr 3.227f.
44:27–45:1	SibOr 3.285
45:2	ApZeph 5:5
45:5	SibOr 3.628
45:5	2En 36:1
45:5	2En 47:3
45:5	SibOr 8.377
45:5-6	2En 33:8
45:5f.	ApAdam 2:5
45:7	SibOr 5.173 ftnt q2
45:11	4Ezra 8:7
45:14	SibOr 3.628

46:2	ApEl 5:11 ftnt 2	57:15	3En 1:5 ftnt h
46:4	3En 4:6	57:15	3En 35:6 ftnt j
46:9	2En 33:8	57:16	3En 43:3
46:9	2En 36:1	58:1	4Ezra 1:5
46:9	2En 47:3	58:1-11	ApEl 1:16 ftnt c3
46:10	2En 33:4	58:7	2En 9:1
47:1	SibOr 3.356f.	58:7	2En 63:1
47:5	SibOr 5.436	58:7	SibOr 2.82
47:8	SibOr 5.173	59:14f.	4Ezra 5:10
47:8f.	SibOr 3.77	59:16	3En 48A:6
47:8f.	SibOr 11.290 ftnt j3	59:17	3En 28:8
47:9	SibOr 5.169	59:17	ApEl 4:30
47:12	SibOr 3.225	60:1	SibOr 3.787
48:11	3En 48A:9	60:1	SibOr 14.214
48:13	3En 44:7	60:1-3	ApEl 3:3
49:1	SibOr 3.710	60:1-3	TLevi 4:2
49:3	2Bar 70:10	60:17	3En 45:2 ftnt i
49:3	3En 10:3 ftnt g	60:20	4Ezra 2:35
49:6	SibOr 14.214	60:21	4Ezra 8:7
49:6	TLevi 14:3 ftnt b	60:21	2Bar 84:3
49:10	ApEl 5:6	61:11	TJud 24:2 ftnt b
49:10	ApEl 1:10 ftnt f2	62:3	3En 22:9
49:16	2Bar 4:2	62:3	GkApEzra 6:17 ftnt f
50:1	2Bar 3:2	63:5	3En 48A:8
50:2	4Ezra 8:23	63:8-9 (LXX)	ApEl 1:5 ftnt u
50:2	2Bar 21:6 ftnt c	63:12	3En 48A:3
50:6	SibOr 8.290	63:15	TMos 10:3
51:5	SibOr 3.710	63:16	TJob 33:3 ftnt g
51:9	3En 48A:3	64:8	TJob 33:3 ftnt g
51:9f.	4Ezra 6:50	65:17	1En 72:2
51:10	4Ezra 8:23	65:17	2Bar 32:7
51:16	4Ezra 15:2	65:17	ApEl 5:38 ftnt q3
51:17	SibOr Frag 3.39	65:25	SibOr 3.788
52:10	3En 48A:10	65:25	3Bar 4:3 (Slav.) ftnt e
53:2-3	SibOr 8.257	66:1	1En 84:2
53:6	SibOr 3.721	66:1	SibOr 1.139
53:7	4Ezra 15:10	66:1-2	SibOr 4.8
54:1	4Ezra 2:2	66:12	2Bar 72:3 ftnt b
54:1	2Bar 10:14	66:16	3En 32:1
54:1	ApEl 2:38	66:16	SibOr 3.287
54:9f.	SibOr 1.318	66:16	SibOr 3.761
55:8f.	4Ezra 4:13	66:16	SibOr 4.173 ftnt f2
55:10	2En 5:2 ftnt e	66:16	3En 32:1 ftnt c
55:11	3En 48C:10-11	66:19-21	2Bar 72:3 ftnt b
55:13	2En 47:4	66:20	3En 48A:10
57:1	1En 81:9	66:22	1En 72:2
57:15	3En 35:6	66:24	GkApEzra 1:24
57:15	ApZeph 2:9	66:24	GkApEzra 4:19

Isaiah (cont.)

66:24	TJob 20:8 ftnt f
66:24	VisEzra 35

Jeremiah

1:1-3	2Bar 1:1f.
1:9	4Ezra 15:2
1:15	SibOr 3.667
1:18	2Bar 2:1
2:5	2Bar 14:5
2:28	ApEl 5:11 ftnt z
3:19	ApocEzek Frag 2
3:22	3En 16:5
4:19	TZeb 2:5
5:19	SibOr 3.275
5:22	2En 28:4
6:13	2Bar 77:2
6:14	2Bar 48:32
6:19	2Bar 1:1f.
6:29	TAb 12:14 ftnt g
7:31	SibOr 2.292 ftnt x2
8:1f.	ApDan 8:2 ftnt b
8:2	SibOr 3.227f.
8:10	2Bar 77:2
8:11	2Bar 48:32
8:16-17	TDan 5:6 ftnt b
9:1	2Bar 35:2
9:16	TLevi 10:4 ftnt c
9:17	3En 15:1 ftnt b
9:19 (20)	TJob 25:1 ftnt a
10:2	1En 48:3 ftnt d
10:2	1En 72:12 ftnt y
10:11	2En 2:2
10:12	3En 44:7
10:12	2Bar 21:4
10:13	3En 37:2
10:13	3En 23:11
11:20	2Bar 48:39
13:11	ApocEzek Frag 5
14:9	2Bar 21:22
14:21	2Bar 46:4
15:1	3En 48A:8
15:16	2Bar 21:22
15:20	2Bar 2:1
16:11	SibOr 3.275
16:17	2En 66:5
17:8	ApAdam 6:2
17:9	2Bar 83:3
17:10	2Bar 48:39
17:12	3En 24:22
17:12	2Bar 46:4
19:3	2Bar 1:1f.
20:14	2Bar 10:6
21:8-14	TAsh 1:3 ftnt a
22:3	2En 9:1
22:3	2En 42:9
22:8	ApEl 4:13 ftnt w
22:9	ApEl 1:13
22:29	2Bar 6:8
23:3	2Bar 78:7
23:5	TJud 24:4 ftnt c
23:19	3En 33:5
23:23	ApocEzek Frag 5
24:7	4Ezra 1:29
25:11	SibOr 3.280
25:11-12	TMos 3:14 ftnt g
25:15	SibOr Frag 3.39
25:20	2Bar 42:4 ftnt d
25:27	SibOr 3.356f.
25:30	TMos 10:3
27:18-22	TMos 3:2
29:10	TMos 3:14 ftnt g
30:23	3En 35:5
31:31	TBenj 10:11
31:31	ApEl 1:13 ftnt r2
31:34	2Bar 77:2
31:34	ApEl 5:4 ftnt m
32:12-16	2Bar 1:1f.
32:17	2Bar 54:2
32:27	2Bar 54:2
32:31	2Bar 1:1f.
32:35	TSol 26:1f.
32:35	SibOr 2.292 ftnt x2
33:15	TJud 24:4 ftnt c
33:22	GkApEzra 2:32
34:2	2Bar 8:2
36:4	2Bar 1:1f.
36:8	2Bar 1:1f.
36:14	2Bar 1:1f.
36:32	2Bar 1:1f.
37:11-16	2Bar 2:1 ftnt a
38:1	2Bar 5:7
38:7-13	3Bar Introduction:2 (Gk.) ftnt g
38:23	2Bar 2:1 ftnt a
39:5	2Bar 8:5

39:9	2Bar 8:5	1:15	3En 25:5
39:14	2Bar 9:2	1:15-25	ApAb 18:12
39:15-18	3Bar Introduction:2	1:16	3En 2:2
	(Gk.) ftnt g	1:16	3En 21:3
40:6	2Bar 9:2	1:17	3En 9:5
40:14	2Bar 5:7	1:18	3En 18:25
43:3-6	2Bar 1:1f.	1:18	3En 22:9
43:6-7	2Bar 10:2 ftnt a	1:18	3En 25:6
45:1	2Bar 1:1f.	1:18	3En 26:5
48:26	SibOr 3.356f.	1:22	3En 44:7
49:1f.	TSol 26:1f.	1:23	ApAb 18:3
49:7	TJob 29:3 ftnt a	1:24	TAdam 1:5
50:1f.	SibOr 3.302	1:25	3En 22C:5
50:12	2Bar 3:2	1:26	1En 14:18
50:12f.	ApEl 2:52	1:26	1En 18:8
51:1f.	SibOr 5.434f.	1:26-28	ApAb 18:14
51:15	2Bar 21:4	1:28	3En 21:4
51:59	2Bar 1:1f.	2:1	2Bar 13:2
51:59	2Bar 5:5	3:12	3En 1:12
51:59	TSol 8:6 ftnt e	3:12	3En 48B:2
51:61	2Bar 5:5	3:16-21	ApocEzek Frag 2
52:17	TSol 21:4	5:5	1En 26:2
52:19	ApEl 2:43 ftnt d3	5:12	SibOr 3.544
		6:1	ApEl 1:1
Lamentations		7:11	3En 31:2 ftnt e
2:15	TJob 29:4 ftnt b	7:19	ApEl 1:19
3:23	3En 40:4	8:8-16	TMos 2:9
3:23	3En 46:1 ftnt b	8:10	SibOr 3.589
3:23	3En 46:4 (14 sic)	9:2	TLevi 8:2 ftnt b
		9:17	SibOr 3.31
Ezekiel		9:17	SibOr 5.356
1:1	2Bar 22:1	10:1	3En 22:12
1:1-3	2Bar 1:1f.	10:1	3En 22:16
1:1f.	2En 1a:4 ftnt j	10:2	3En 24:16
1:1f.	2En 20:1	10:3	3En 19:1
1:1f.	3En 1:1	10:5	3En 22:15
1:1f.	GkApEzra 2:26 ftnt l	10:6-12	ApAb 18:12
1:1f.	TLevi 2:5 ftnt c	10:12	3En 24:18
1:5	3En 21:1	10:12	2En 1a:4 ftnt i
1:5-11	2En 12:1 ftnt f	10:12f.	3En 25:5
1:6-12	ApAb 18:3	10:13	3En 25:5 ftnt g
1:9	1En 14:18	10:14	3En 2:1 ftnt a
1:10	TNaph 5:6 ftnt c	11:1	ApZeph A
1:10	3En 2:1 ftnt a	11:1f.	TNaph 5:3 ftnt b
1:10	3En 15B:2 ftnt h	11:23	TNaph 5:2 ftnt a
1:10	3En 26:3 ftnt d	12:1	ApEl 1:1
1:14	3En 22C:5	12:15	TLevi 10:4 ftnt c
1:14	3En 24:15	13:1	ApEl 1:1

Ezekiel (cont.)

13:10	2Bar 48:32
13:11	3En 34:1 ftnt e
13:13	3En 34:1 ftnt e
14:2	ApEl 1:1
15:1	3Bar 1:2
16:20	TMos 2:8
17:3	TNaph 5:6 ftnt c
17:3-9	2Bar 36:2
18:3	3En 1:2
18:7	2En 9:1
18:7	2En 63:1
18:8	2En 42:7
18:30	ApocEzek Frag 4
18:31	ApocEzek Frag 2
19:9 (LXX)	TJob 27:1 ftnt b
20:26	TMos 2:8
20:39	ApAb 29:16 ftnt n
21:3	3En 32:1 ftnt c
22:9	ApEl 1:13
24:14	2En 33:4
25:13	TJob 29:3 ftnt a
26:7	TMos 8:1
27:32-36	TJob 25:1 ftnt a
28:1f.	2En 29:3 ftnt i
28:2	SibOr 5.173
28:12 (LXX)	GkApEzra 6:17 ftnt f
28:13	2En 8:3 ftnt f
28:16	2En 29:3 ftnt f
31:8	2En 8:7
33:1f.	ApEl 1:1
33:12-20	ApocEzek Frag 4
34:1f.	ApEl 5:31 ftnt d3
34:14-16	ApocEzek Frag 5
37:1	3En 23:7
37:1-10	SibOr 2.224
37:1-10	SibOr 4.181
38:1	SibOr 3.319
38:1f.	SibOr 3.663f.
38:2	3En 45:5
38:5	SibOr 3.323 ftnt i2
38:12	1En 26:1
38:20	SibOr 3.677
38:22	SibOr 3.287
38:22	SibOr 3.690
38:23	SibOr 3.693
39:6	3En 45:5
39:9	SibOr 3.649

39:9	SibOr 5.381
39:9f.	SibOr 3.727
39:22	ApocEzek Frag 2
40:1f.–ch. 48	GkApEzra 2:22 ftnt i
42:20	1En 77:1f.
43:1f.	TNaph 5:3 ftnt b
43:2	TNaph 5:2 ftnt a
44:11	3En 45:2 ftnt i
45:1	3En 2:3 ftnt e
45:18	ApAb 11:3 ftnt b
47:12	1En 25:5 ftnt g
47:12	TLevi 9:12 ftnt d
48:35	3En 24:17
53:11 (sic)	TAb rec. A 10:14

Daniel

1:8-16	TJos 3:4
1:17	TLevi 2:3 ftnt b
2:2	TNaph 5:6 ftnt c
2:4	4Ezra 13:6
2:14	2En 33:11
2:21	3En 48C:9
2:22 (LXX)	TJob 37:6 ftnt d
2:22	SibOr Frag 3.34
2:28	TJob 1:4 ftnt j
2:34	4Ezra 13:37
2:37	TMos 8:1
2:44	SibOr 3.767
2:44	SibOr 14.361
2:45	TJob 1:4 ftnt j
2:45	4Ezra 13:37
3:8	TNaph 5:6 ftnt c
4:7	TNaph 5:6 ftnt c
4:10	3En 28:1 ftnt a
4:10	SibOr 1.98 ftnt f
4:10f. (MT)	3En 28:9
4:13	1En 1:5
4:13	3En 28:1
4:14	SibOr 1.98 ftnt f
4:14	3En 28:1 ftnt a
4:17	1En 1:5
4:17	3En 28:1
4:17	3En 28:4
4:17	3En 28:9
4:20	SibOr 1.98 ftnt f
4:23	1En 1:5
4:25 (LXX)	TLevi 5:7 ftnt e
5:6	2En 1:7

5:7	TNaph 5:6 ftnt c	7:27	SibOr 14.361
5:9	2En 1:7	7:27	2Bar 40:3
5:10	2En 1:7	8:5-8	TNaph 5:6
5:12	1En 8:3	8:10	SibOr 5.212 ftnt y2
5:27	2En 49:2 ftnt b	8:10f.	SibOr 1.314
6:1f.	QuesEzra 40	8:15	2En 1:4
6:1f.	TJos 8:5 ftnt a	8:16	TSol 18:6
6:10	2En 51:4	8:16	3En 14:4
6:10	ApZeph 7:6	8:17	ApZeph 6:5
7:1–ch. 8	SibOr 13.158 ftnt h2	8:17f.	3En 1:7
7:1–ch. 8	SibOr 14.12 ftnt a	8:20	TSol 15:8
7:1f.	2Bar 39:5 ftnt a	9:1	TSol 15:8
7:1f.	SibOr 2.219 ftnt q2	9:1-27	TLevi 15:1 ftnt a
7:1f.	SibOr 8.88 ftnt m	9:1f.	TJud 23:4 ftnt a
7:3	4Ezra 11:1	9:3	ApEl 1:13 ftnt q2
7:5	3En 26:12 ftnt m	9:4-19	TMos 4:1
7:7	SibOr 3.329	9:11	3En 44:9
7:7	SibOr 3.398	9:13	TMos 3:13
7:7	4Ezra 12:10 ftnt b	9:21	TSol 18:6
7:8	SibOr 3.400	9:21	TMos 3:14 ftnt g
7:8	SibOr 5.222	9:23	3Bar 11:7 (Gk.) ftnt e
7:8	TJos 19:8 ftnt c	9:24	TNaph 6:1 ftnt a
7:9	1En 14:18	9:27	ApEl 3:5 ftnt j
7:9	3En 28:7	9:27 (LXX)	TReu 6:8 ftnt c
7:9	ApZeph A ftnt c	10:1f.–ch. 11	TNaph 5:6 ftnt c
7:9	ApAb 11:3	10:5f.	ApZeph 6:13
7:9-10	QuesEzra (rec. A) 20	10:6	2En 1:5
7:9-10	SibOr 8.82	10:6	3En 35:2
7:9-14	TLevi 2:10 ftnt e	10:9	3En 1:7
7:9f.	2Bar 21:6	10:10	3En 1:7
1 Dan 7:10 (sic)	2Bar 24:1	10:10	ApZeph 6:5
7:10	1En 14:18	10:11 (Theodotion)	3Bar 1:3 ftnt e
7:10	2En 10:2	10:13	TSol 1:6
7:10	3En 18:19	10:13	TSol 18:5
7:10	3En 30:2	10:13	TMos 10:2 ftnt a
7:10	3En 35:4	10:13	3Bar 11:4 (Gk.) ftnt c
7:10	3En 22B:3	10:13	TLevi 5:6 ftnt d
7:10	ApZeph 3:8 ftnt g	10:15	3En 1:7
7:10	ApZeph 4:1f.	10:17	2Bar 22:1
7:10	4Ezra 6:20	10:20f.	TSol 1:6
7:13	SibOr 5.256	10:20f.	TSol 18:5
7:13-14	4Ezra 12:32	10:21	TLevi 5:6 ftnt d
7:15	2En 1:3 ftnt e	10:21	3Bar 11:4 (Gk.) ftnt c
7:15	2En 22:8 ftnt m	10:21	TMos 10:2 ftnt a
7:22 (LXX)	TAb 13:6 ftnt c	11:1f.	TNaph 5:6 ftnt c
7:25	SibOr 5.155 ftnt m2	11:29	2Bar 1:1f.
7:25	ApEl 2:52	11:31	ApEl 3:5 ftnt j
7:27	SibOr 3.767	11:33	ApEl 1:13 ftnt n2

Daniel (cont.)

		2:9-10	TLevi 10:3 ftnt b
11:33	ApEl 2:15	4:5	2Bar 3:2
11:35	ApEl 1:13 ftnt n2	5:10	ApEl 1:4 ftnt r
11:35	2Bar 1:1f.	6:2f.	3En 28:10
11:36-39	ApEl 1:2 ftnt g	6:6	SibOr 2.82
11:40	ApEl 2:3	6:6	SibOr 8.334
11:43	SibOr 5.222 ftnt a3	10:8	ApEl 2:33
12:1	3En 18:6	10:13	2En 42:11
12:1	3En 44:10	11:1	SibOr 3.702
12:1	TMos 8:1	11:9	TLevi 5:2
12:1	TMos 10:2 ftnt a	14:5	4Ezra 5:24
12:1	TSol 1:6	14:5-7	TSim 6:2 ftnt a
12:1	TSol 18:5		
12:1	TAb 12:12 ftnt d	*Joel*	
12:1	ApZeph 3:8 ftnt g	1:14	ApEl 1:16 ftnt c3
12:1	TLevi 5:6 ftnt d	2:5	ApEl 1:5
12:1	4Ezra 6:20	2:10	SibOr 3.801
12:1 (Theodotion)	TAb 1:4 ftnt b	2:13	GkApEzra 1:10
12:1f.	ApZeph 5:4 ftnt a		ftnt m
12:1f.	3En 18:24 ftnt l2	2:15	ApEl 1:16 ftnt c3
12:2	TJud 25:4	2:17	4Ezra 8:45
12:2	TBenj 10:7	2:17	3Bar 1:2
12:2	TSim 6:7 ftnt d	2:28-29	TJud 24:2
12:2	4Ezra 7:32	2:30	ApEl 1:4 ftnt r
12:3	4Ezra 7:97	2:31	ApEl 3:7
12:3	4Ezra 7:125	2:32	TJob 33:5 ftnt i
12:3	ApAdam 7:52	3:1	SibOr 3.293
12:3	2Bar 51:10 ftnt c	3:1	TJud 24:2 ftnt b
12:3	ApEl 1:13 ftnt n2	4:2	GkApEzra 3:5
12:3	ApEl 4:19	4:12	GkApEzra 3:5
12:3	TMos 10:9 ftnt f		
12:3	TLevi 4:2	*Amos*	
12:4	SibOr 11.170 ftnt m2	1:12	TJob 29:3 ftnt a
12:4	ApZeph 5:6 ftnt b	1:15	TSol 26:1f.
12:4 (LXX)	TReu 6:8 ftnt c	4:13	3En 23:18
12:5	4Ezra 7:125	5:8	TSol 8:2 ftnt a
12:7	SibOr 5.122 ftnt m2	5:18	SibOr 3.741
12:9	SibOr 11.170 ftnt m2	5:18	SibOr 11.45
12:10	2Bar 28:1	5:26	TSol 26:2 ftnt b
12:11	ApEl 3:5 ftnt j	5:26	TSol 15:5
12:12	4Ezra 7:32	5:26	TSol 26:1f.
12:13 (LXX)	TReu 6:8 ftnt c	7:4	SibOr 4.173 ftnt f2
		9:1	3En 24:5

Hosea

		Obadiah	
1:1	2Bar 1:1f.	8-9	TJob 29:3 ftnt a
2:8	SibOr 3.243		
2:8	SibOr 3.745		
2:8 (10)	SibOr 8.382		

Jonah
1:15	3En 14:3 ftnt c
1:17 (LXX)	TZeb 4:4
2:4	SibOr 2.240 ftnt t2
2:6	SibOr 2.240 ftnt t2

Micah
1:3	1En 1:4
1:3	TMos 10:3
1:3-4	SibOr 8.433
1:4	SibOr 3.680
1:4	4Ezra 8:23
1:4	4Ezra 13:4
1:8 (LXX)	2Bar 10:8
3:11	TLevi 14:6
4:2	SibOr 3.718
4:2	SibOr 3.772
5:1f.	SibOr 8.479
6:2	ApEl 5:25 ftnt v2
6:6-8	2En 45:3
7:6	SibOr 8.84
7:6	3Bar 4:17
7:10	3Bar 1:2

Habakkuk
2:4	2Bar 54:17
2:5	2Bar 56:6
2:11	4Ezra 5:5
3:3	3En 18:18
3:6	SibOr 3.675
3:6	SibOr 8.433
3:10	2En 33:4 ftnt f
3:15	SibOr 1.315 ftnt a2
3:15	SibOr 5.157 ftnt n2

Zephaniah
1:1-6	ApZeph 3:4 ftnt c
1:10-13	ApZeph 2:1 ftnt b
1:15	ApZeph 12:5
1:15	ApEl 1:19
1:17	ApZeph 10:8
1:18	ApEl 1:19
1:18	ApEl 1:4 ftnt r
1:23	ApEl 1:4 ftnt r
2:3	ApEl 1:19
3:5	3En 26:6

Haggai
1:1f.	SibOr 3.290
2:6	TLevi 3:9 ftnt e
2:6-7	TLevi 3:10
2:9	TBenj 9:2
2:21-22	TLevi 3:10

Zechariah
1:7-11	TAdam 4:7
1:8	3En 17:8
1:8	3En 18:1
1:8	2Bar 36:1
1:12	TMos 4:1 ftnt a
2:5	SibOr 3.706
2:5-9	GkApEzra 2:22 ftnt i
2:10	SibOr 3.785
2:16	TJob 33:5 ftnt i
3:1	3En 14:1
3:1f.	3En 26:12
3:4-5	2En 22:8
3:4-5	ApEl 5:6 ftnt p
3:5	ApAb 11:3 ftnt b
3:8 (LXX)	TSol 9:6 ftnt c
3:8	TJud 24:4 ftnt c
4:14	TGad 8:1 ftnt a
6:12	TJud 24:4 ftnt c
6:12 (LXX)	TSol 9:6 ftnt c
7:9	2En 42:7
7:10	2En 42:9
7:10	2En 50:6
7:11	2Bar 51:5
7:14	TLevi 10:4 ftnt c
8:16	2En 42:12
8:16f.	TDan 5:2
9:4	GkApEzra 4:36 ftnt n
9:9	SibOr 8.325
9:9	TDan 6:9
11:12	TGad 2:3 ftnt a
12:1	2En 47:4
13:8	SibOr 3.544
13:8	SibOr 5.103
13:9	4Ezra 16:73
13:9	TAb 12:14 ftnt g
14:1f.	TNaph 5:2 ftnt a
14:4	4Ezra 5:8 ftnt h
14:4-7	TNaph 5:1
14:9	3En 48A:10

Zechariah (cont.)
14:9   ApEl 2:11
14:16   SibOr 3.772

Malachi
1:6   TJob 33:3 ftnt g
2:10   TJob 33:3 ftnt g
3:2   SibOr Frag 8.4
3:2   ApZeph 12:6
3:2   TAb 12:14 ftnt g
3:2   TAb 13:4 ftnt a
3:5   TJob 12:4 ftnt b

3:16   4Ezra 6:20
3:16   ApZeph 3:8 ftnt g
3:19   ApEl 1:4 ftnt p
3:23   SibOr 2.187f.
4:1   ApEl 1:4
4:2   SibOr 3.94
4:2   TJud 24:1 ftnt a
4:2   TZeb 9:8
4:4   3En 48D:4
4:5   ApEl 4:7 ftnt m
4:5   ApDan 14:2 ftnt b

NEW TESTAMENT

Matthew
1:1   TSol 1:7
1:1   TSol 20:2
1:1-14   ApAdam 7:45 ftnt q
1:9   ApZeph 3:4 ftnt c
1:18   2En 71:2 ftnt c
1:18-25   TIsaac 3:17
1:18-25   TSol 22:20
1:20   TSol 1:7
1:20   TSol 20:2
1:23   TSol 6:8
1:23   TSol 11:6
1:23   TSol 15:12
2:2   SibOr 8.476
2:2   SibOr 12.30
2:11   TJob 32:10 ftnt m
2:11   SibOr 1.334
2:16   GkApEzra 4:11
2:16   VisEzra 38
2:16   ApDan 1:10
2:20   SibOr 1.345
3:1-6   SibOr 1.336f.
3:1-6   SibOr 4.165
3:7   SibOr 8.1
3:10 par   ApAdam 6:2
3:16   2Bar 22:2
3:16   ApEl 3:2
3:16-17   SibOr 6.4
4:8   2Bar 76:3
4:10   TJob 26:3 ftnt d
5:5   TJob 33:5 ftnt i
5:8   2En 45:3
5:8   4Ezra 7:98
5:9   2En 52:10

5:10   2Bar 52:6 ftnt b
5:17   SibOr 1.332
5:22   2En 44:2
5:22   SibOr 2.292
5:22   SibOr 2.292 ftnt x2
5:29   1En 27:2
5:30   1En 27:2
5:34   2En 49:1 ftnt a
5:34-35   2En 49:1
6:2f.   VisEzra 3
6:13   TJob 43:5 ftnt e
6:16-18   ApEl 1:13 ftnt q2
6:19   TAb 10:10 ftnt e
6:19-20   2Bar 14:13
6:20f.   TLevi 13:5
6:22   TIss 4:6
7:2   2En 44:4
7:2   TZeb 8:3
7:7   SibOr 7.90
7:13   2Bar 85:13
7:13   TAb 11:11 ftnt f
7:13f.   TAb rec. B 8:16 ftnt e
7:13f.   TAb 11:2 ftnt b
7:13-14   TAsh 1:3 ftnt a
7:15   SibOr 7.134
7:16-20 par   ApAdam 6:2
8:11   TLevi 18:14 ftnt f
8:11   3En 48A:10 ftnt x
8:12   SibOr 8.86
8:12   SibOr 8.231
8:12   TJac 5:9
8:12   GkApEzra 4:37 ftnt o
8:26   2Bar 21:6 ftnt c
8:29   1En 16:1

9:13	SibOr 2.82	13:43	TLevi 4:2
9:13	SibOr 8.334	14:3-12	SibOr 1.343
9:13	ApSedr 15:1	14:12	SibOr 2.202
9:27	TSol 1:7	14:13-21	SibOr 1.357f.
9:27	TSol 20:2	14:23-33	SibOr 1.356
9:34	TSol 2:9	14:25	ApEl 2:6 ftnt p
9:36	ApEl 4:1 ftnt a	14:26	SibOr 6.12f.
10:16	ApEl 3:2 ftnt e	14:27	2En 1:7
10:21	3Bar 4:17	15:17	TJob 38:3 ftnt d
10:25	TSol 2:9	15:22	TSol 1:7
10:25	TSol 3:1	15:22	TSol 20:2
10:35-36	SibOr 8.84	15:30f.	SibOr 8.272
10:42	2Bar 48:19	16:14	SibOr 2.187f.
11:2-6	SibOr 1.350	16:19	3Bar 11:2 ftnt b
11:5	ApEl 3:9	16:23	TJob 26:3 ftnt d
11:5	SibOr 6.12f.	16:26	2Bar 51:16
11:5	SibOr 8.205	16:27	SibOr 2.240f.
11:7	SibOr 8.297	16:27	ApEl 3:4 ftnt i
11:14	SibOr 2.187f.	17:2	2Bar 51:3
11:29	2En 34:1	17:2	ApZeph 5:4 ftnt a
11:29	SibOr 8.326	17:5	1En 14:8
12:7	SibOr 2.82	17:5 par	2Bar 22:2
12:23	TSol 1:7	17:10	SibOr 2.187f.
12:23	TSol 20:2	18:6	2Bar 48:19
12:24	TSol 2:9	18:10	2Bar 48:19
12:24	TSol 3:1	18:22	TBenj 7:4 ftnt b
12:39-40	ApEl 3:2 ftnt e	19:28	TJob 33:1 ftnt a
12:40	TZeb 4:4	19:28	SibOr 2.219 ftnt q2
12:42	TSol 19:3	19:28	TAb 13:6 ftnt c
12:42	TSol 21:1	19:28-30	TBenj 10:7
12:43	TSol 7:7 ftnt e	19:29	SibOr Frag 3.47
12:45	TSol 8:2 ftnt a	19:29	3Bar 15:2 (Gk.) ftnt b
13:1-9 par	GkApEzra 5:12 ftnt d	20:20	TSol 1:7
13:13-15	SibOr 1.360f.	20:20	TSol 20:2
13:17	2Bar 85:2	20:21	TJob 33:1 ftnt a
13:19	TJob 43:5 ftnt e	20:31	TSol 1:7
13:22	QuesEzra 37	20:31	TSol 20:2
13:36-43	SibOr 1.387	21:5	SibOr 8.325
13:39	TJob 4:6 ftnt b	21:9	TSol 1:7
13:39	TReu 6:8 ftnt c	21:9	TSol 20:2
13:42	SibOr 8.231	21:13	SibOr 2.150
13:42	VisEzra 59 d6	21:15	TSol 1:7
13:43	ApEl 4:19 ftnt g2	21:15	TSol 20:2
13:43	2En 22:10	21:42	TSol 22:8
13:43	2En 65:8	21:42	TSol 23:4
13:43	2En 65:11	22:2	ApocEzek Frag 1 1:2
13:43	4Ezra 7:97	22:2	ApocEzek Frag 3
13:43	ApAdam 7:52		ftnt b

Matthew (cont.)

22:13	TJac 5:9
22:13	GkApEzra 4:37 ftnt o
22:14	TAb 11:12 ftnt g
22:29-33	ApZeph 5:5 ftnt a
22:30	2En 22:10 ftnt p
22:37-39	SibOr 8.481
22:40	ApSedr 1:13
23:1-3	VisEzra 46
23:34	SibOr 2.247
23:37	SibOr 2.247
23:37	4Ezra 1:30
24:1	4Ezra 5:2
24:5	ApEl 3:1
24:4	ApEl 1:14
24:6	2Bar 48:34
24:6	2Bar 48:37
24:6f.	SibOr 3.636f.
24:7	2En 70:23
24:7	SibOr 1.397
24:7	SibOr 2.6f.
24:7	SibOr 2.23
24:7	4Ezra 13:31
24:7	4Ezra 15:15
24:7 (1 sic)	2Bar 27:9 ftnt a
24:8	2Bar 27:3
24:11	SibOr 2.166
24:11	2Bar 48:34
24:11	ApEl 1:13 ftnt o2
24:15	2Bar 28:1
24:15	ApEl 3:5 ftnt j
24:16-20	ApEl 4:24 ftnt o2
24:17	2Bar 53:9
24:19	SibOr 2.190f.
24:19	2Bar 10:14
24:19	ApDan 12:6 ftnt j
24:21	TMos 8:1
24:24	SibOr 2.166
24:24	2Bar 48:34
24:27	SibOr 6.18
24:27	ApEl 3:4
24:27	ApEl 3:10 ftnt r
24:29	SibOr 2.202
24:29	ApEl 3:6
24:30	SibOr 2.240f.
24:30	2Bar 25:3
24:30	ApEl 3:3 ftnt g
24:30	ApEl 5:36 ftnt o3
24:31	1En 22:3
24:31	SibOr 8.239
24:31	QuesEzra rec. B 13
24:31	GkApEzra 4:36 ftnt n
24:34	2En 23:4 ftnt f
24:37	2Bar 30:1 ftnt a
24:37	2En 70:10 ftnt n
24:40f.	ApZeph 2:2
24:43	TAb 10:10 ftnt e
24:45-51	SibOr 2.180f.
25:1-13	SibOr 2.180f.
25:23	3Bar 15:4
25:30	GkApEzra 4:37 ftnt o
25:31	SibOr 2.240f.
25:31-46	TJos 1:5
25:31-46	2En 9:1 ftnt b
25:32f.	SibOr 8.417
25:34	2En 9:1
25:34	2En 23:5
25:34	2En 42:3
25:34	4Ezra 2:13
25:34	2En 9:1 ftnt f
25:35	2En 9:1
25:35	TIsaac 6:21
25:36	VisEzra 6
25:37	2En 9:1
25:41	1En 10:13
25:41	2En 10:4
25:46	2En 46:3 ftnt d
25:46	TAb 11:11 ftnt f
26:14f.	ApDan 9:7
26:15	TGad 2:3 ftnt a
26:24	2Bar 10:6
26:39	SibOr 3.655
26:53	TSol 11:3
26:64	3En 28:1 ftnt a
26:64	TJob 33:3 ftnt g
27:3	TGad 2:3 ftnt a
27:22	TSol 12:3
27:24f.	TLevi 16:3
27:27-31	SibOr 1.374
27:29	SibOr 6.24
27:34	SibOr 1.368
27:34	SibOr 6.24
27:34	GkApEzra 2:25
27:34	GkApEzra 7:1
27:39	TJob 29:4 ftnt b
27:42	ApEl 5:11 ftnt z

27:45	SibOr 1.374	9:49	TLevi 9:14
27:46	TSol 6:8	10:17	SibOr Frag 3.47
27:51	SibOr 1.376	10:20	2Bar 38:4
27:51	GkApEzra 4:36 ftnt n	10:30	3Bar 15:2 (Gk.) ftnt b
		10:47f.	TSol 1:7
Mark		10:47f.	TSol 20:1
1:1-6	SibOr 1.336f.	11:18	TLevi 16:3
1:4f.	SibOr 4.165	12:1	TJos 19:12 ftnt d
1:9-11	SibOr 6.4	12:10	TSol 22:7
1:9-11	TLevi 18:7 ftnt c	12:10	TSol 23:4
1:13	TJob 40:11 ftnt i	12:29-31	SibOr 8.481
1:13	TJob 20:9 ftnt g	12:35	TSol 1:7
1:13	TNaph 8:4 ftnt b	12:35	TSol 20:1
1:34	ApEl 5:32 ftnt j3	12:36	ApEl 4:28
2:18-20	ApEl 1:13 ftnt q2	13:3f.	TNaph 5:2 ftnt a
3:22	TSol 2:9	13:4	2Bar 25:3
3:22	TSol 3:1	13:5	ApEl 1:14
3:27	TLevi 18:12 ftnt e	13:5	2Bar 27:2 ftnt a
4:12	SibOr 1.360f.	13:7	ApEl 2:2
4:35-41	SibOr 8.273	13:7f.	ApDan 1:1
5:1-13	TSol 11:3 ftnt c	13:8	SibOr 1.397
5:5	TSol 1:13	13:8	SibOr 2.6f.
5:9	TSol 11:3	13:8	SibOr 2.23
5:13	TSol 5:12	13:8	SibOr 3.636f.
5:13	TSol 11:6	13:8	4Ezra 15:15
5:15	TSol 11:3	13:8	2Bar 27:9
6:11	2Bar 13:4	13:9 par	2Bar 13:4
6:17-29	SibOr 1.342	13:12	3Bar 4:17
6:30-44	SibOr 1.357f.	13:14	ApEl 3:5 ftnt j
6:45-51	SibOr 1.356	13:14-19	ApEl 4:24 ftnt o2
6:48	SibOr 6.12f.	13:17	SibOr 2.190f.
6:48	ApEl 3:8	13:17	ApDan 12:6 ftnt j
6:48-52	SibOr 8.273	13:22	SibOr 2.166
7:19	TJob 38:3 ftnt d	13:22	ApAdam 6:5
8:1-10	SibOr 1.357f.	13:24 par	ApAdam 5:10
8:33	TJob 26:3 ftnt d	13:25	SibOr 2.202
8:38	SibOr 2.240f.	13:26	SibOr 2.240f.
8:38	ApEl 3:4 ftnt i	13:32	GkApEzra 3:5 ftnt a
9:2	ApZeph 5:4 ftnt a	14:1	TLevi 16:3
9:18	TSol 12:2	14:36	ApocEzek Frag 2
9:20	TSol 12:2	14:58	2Bar 4:2
9:26	TSol 1:13 ftnt q	15:16-20	SibOr 1.374
9:29	ApEl 1:21 ftnt l3	15:18	SibOr 6.24
9:39	TSol 1:13	15:22	TSol 12:3
9:45	3En 44:3	15:23	SibOr 6.24
9:48	GkApEzra 4:19	15:31	ApEl 5:11 ftnt z
9:48	VisEzra 34	15:33	SibOr 1.374
9:48	TJob 20:8 ftnt f	15:34	TSol 6:8

Mark (cont.)

15:36	GkApEzra 2:25
15:36	GkApEzra 7:1
15:38	SibOr 1.376
15:39	TSol 15:10 ftnt f
16:18	TJos 6:2 ftnt a
16:19	TJob 33:3 ftnt g

Luke

1:6	2En 9:1
1:6	ApZeph 3:4
1:14-17	TJob 25:1 ftnt a
1:19	TSol 18:6
1:26	SibOr 8.459
1:26-38	TSol 22:20
1:31-36	SibOr 8.462
1:32f.	TJob 25:1 ftnt a
1:34-38	TIsaac 3:17
1:37	2Bar 54:2
1:42	2Bar 54:11
1:52	SibOr 13.3
1:68	SibOr 8.246
1:69	2En 35:2 ftnt e
1:78	TJob 40:3 ftnt b
1:78	TSol 9:6 ftnt c
2:1f.	SibOr 3.372 ftnt o2
2:7f.	SibOr 8.477
2:8	TAb 10:2 ftnt b
2:11	TSol 17:4
2:14	2En 35:1 ftnt a
2:25	2Bar 44:8
2:32	1En 48:4
2:41-52	2En 71:18 ftnt l
3:1-6	SibOr 1.336f.
3:3f.	SibOr 4.165
3:7	SibOr 8.1
3:21-22	SibOr 6.4
3:23	2En 67:1 ftnt a
4:8	TJob 26:3 ftnt d
4:25	ApEl 3:1 ftnt a
4:39	2Bar 21:6 ftnt c
4:41	TSol 1:12 ftnt o
6:38	2En 44:4
6:38	2En 50:5
7:18-23	SibOr 1.350
7:22	SibOr 6.12f.
8:2	TSol 8:2 ftnt a
8:10	SibOr 1.360f.

8:12	ApAdam 6:1 ftnt b
9:5	ApAdam 6:1 ftnt b
9:10-17	SibOr 1.357f.
9:26	SibOr 2.240f.
9:28f.	ApZeph 5:4 ftnt a
9:42	2Bar 21:6 ftnt c
10:18	TBenj 3:7 ftnt b
10:18	2En 29:3 ftnt i
10:19	TLevi 18:12 ftnt e
10:27	SibOr 8.481
10:27	TIss 5:2
11:14-22	TLevi 18:12 ftnt e
11:15	TSol 2:9
11:15	TSol 3:1
11:25	2Bar 25:3
11:26	TSol 8:2 ftnt a
11:27	2Bar 54:11
11:31	TSol 19:3
11:31	TSol 21:1
11:49-51	SibOr 2.247
12:19	TAb rec. B 5:1 ftnt a
12:42-46	SibOr 2.180f.
12:53	SibOr 8.84
13:28	SibOr 8.86
13:28	SibOr 8.231
13:28-29	2En 42:5
13:34	4Ezra 1:30
14:14	2En 50:5
14:16	2En 42:5
14:16	ApocEzek Frag 1 1:2
14:16	ApocEzek Frag 3 ftnt b
15:11-24	ApSedr 6:4
16:9	4Ezra 2:11
16:22	ApSedr 14:6
16:22f.	TAb 20:14 ftnt l
16:23-26	ApEl 5:27 ftnt a3
16:23f.	4Ezra 7:36
16:24	2En 63:4 ftnt e
17:24	SibOr 6.18
17:24	ApEl 3:4
17:26	2En 70:10 ftnt n
17:31-33	ApEl 4:24 ftnt o2
17:34f.	ApZeph 2:2
18:12	ApEl 1:13 ftnt q2
18:18	SibOr Frag 3.47
18:21	2Bar 38:4
19:40	4Ezra 5:5

20:15	ApocEzek Frag 1 2:6	1:31	2Bar 29:3 ftnt b
20:17	TSol 23:4	1:31-32	SibOr 6.4
20:17f.	TSol 22:8	1:51	ApEl 5:39 ftnt s3
20:36	2Bar 51:9	2:11	ApEl 3:12 ftnt s
21:7	2Bar 25:3	2:23	ApEl 3:12 ftnt s
21:10	SibOr 1.397	2:23	TrShem 6:13 ftnt h
21:10	SibOr 2.6f.	3:1f.	2En 1:1 ftnt a
21:10	SibOr 2.23	3:2	ApEl 3:12 ftnt s
21:10	SibOr 3.636f.	3:3	SibOr 1.340
21:10	4Ezra 15:15	3:3	SibOr 8.316
21:10f.	ApDan 1:1 ftnt g	3:7	SibOr 8.316
21:11	2Bar 27:9	3:12	TJob 38:2 ftnt c
21:19	2En 50:2	3:17	ApEl 1:6
21:23	SibOr 2.190f.	3:19	2Bar 18:2
21:23	ApDan 12:6 ftnt g	3:19-21	2En 46:3
21:25-26	2Bar 25:4	3:36	SibOr 8.254
21:26	4Ezra 15:18	4:1f.	SibOr 8.271
21:28	2Bar 23:7	4:48	ApAdam 6:5
21:28	3En 48A:5 ftnt k	4:48	ApEl 5:1 ftnt g
22:27	TJos 17:8	5:20	3Bar 5:3 (Gk.) ftnt c
22:30	3En 48:A:10 ftnt x	5:22	ApEl 5:25 ftnt v2
22:30	TJob 33:1 ftnt a	5:27	ApEl 5:25 ftnt v2
22:69	TJob 33:3 ftnt g	5:30	ApEl 5:24 ftnt u2
23:29	2Bar 10:14	5:35	2En 46:3
23:29	ApEl 2:38	5:35	2Bar 18:2
23:30	ApEl 2:34	6:1-13	SibOr 1.357f.
23:36	SibOr 6.24	6:1f.	TJac 7:23
23:36	GkApEzra 2:25	6:18-21	SibOr 8.273
23:36	GkApEzra 7:1	6:19	SibOr 6.12f.
23:37	ApEl 5:11 ftnt z	6:31-33	SibOr Frag 3.49
23:39	2En 7:1 ftnt e	6:38	SibOr 3.655
23:43	ApSedr 15:2	7:24	VisEzra 39
23:44	SibOr 1.374	8:12	2En 46:3
23:45	SibOr 1.376	8:12	SibOr Frag 1.27
24:4	2En 1:4 ftnt j	8:12	ApDan 14:16
24:4	2En 1:7 ftnt v	8:56	SibOr 6.19 ftnt a
		8:56	TLevi 18:14 ftnt f
John		9:2	TJob 23:6 ftnt d
1:1	2En 33:4	10:36	ApEl 1:6
1:4-9	SibOr Frag 1.27	11:6	TAb 20:11 ftnt f
1:8	2En 46:3	11:39	TAb 20:11 ftnt f
1:9	2Bar 18:2	12:6	3En 27:2 ftnt b
1:14	SibOr 8.470	12:15	SibOr 8.325
1:14	SibOr 12.33	12:31	TSol 2:9
1:14	SibOr 12.232	12:40	SibOr 1.360f.
1:23	SibOr 1.336f.	13:29	3En 27:2 ftnt b
1:29	2En 64:5	14:2	2En 61:2
1:29	TBenj 3:7 ftnt b	14:2	2Bar 48:6

John (cont.)

14:2	TAb 20:14 ftnt k
14:23	1En 45:3
14:30	TSol 2:9
15:1	2Bar 39:7
15:1f.	2En 50:2 ftnt b
15:13	ApSedr 1:25
16:7-13	TJud 20:5
16:11	TSol 2:9
19:17	TSol 12:3
17:12	ApEl 2:40
17:22	TJud 25:3
19:1-3	SibOr 1.374
19:17	TSol 12:3
19:20	TJob 20:7 ftnt e
19:26f.	SibOr 8.291
20:7	ApAb 11:3 ftnt b
20:27	SibOr 8.320
20:29	4Ezra 1:37

Acts

1:9	2En 3:1
1:9	SibOr 1.381
1:9	2En 67:3 ftnt c
1:10	2En 1:4 ftnt j
1:11	TJob 39:12 ftnt e
2:11	2En 54:1
2:11	TJob 38:1 ftnt a
2:15	2En 51:5
2:19	ApEl 5:1 ftnt g
2:22	ApEl 5:1 ftnt g
2:25-36	ApZeph 5:5 ftnt a
2:33	TJob 33:3 ftnt g
2:43	ApEl 5:1 ftnt g
3:1	2En 51:5
3:10	3Bar, Introduction 2 (Gk.) ftnt h
3:12	ApEl 5:4 ftnt l
3:13	2Bar 70:10
3:26	2Bar 70:10
4:11	TSol 22:8
4:11	TSol 23:4
4:24	TJob 2:4 ftnt c
4:27	2Bar 70:10
4:30	ApEl 5:1 ftnt g
5:5	2En 71:9 ftnt i
5:10	2En 71:9 ftnt i
5:30	2En 7:1 ftnt e

5:41	2Bar 52:6 ftnt b
6:1	TJob 10:2 ftnt b
7:2	ApEl 1:5
7:3	ApEl 5:4 ftnt l
7:36-41	TMos 3:11
7:36	TSol 25:4
7:37	TBenj 9:2 ftnt b
7:43	TSol 26:1f.
7:44	SibOr 4.10
7:48f.	SibOr 4.8
7:53	2En 15:1 ftnt a
7:56	SibOr 2.245
7:57	2Bar 22:1
8:10	TSol 2:4 ftnt g
8:38	2Bar 6:4
9:36	VisEzra 3
10:2	VisEzra 3
10:9	2En 51:5
10:39	2En 7:1 ftnt e
12:15	TJob 23:2 ftnt c
12:23	TJob 20:8 ftnt f
13:23	TSol 17:4
14:15	TJob 2:4 ftnt c
15:20	1En 7:5
15:20	SibOr 2.96
15:29	SibOr 2.96
16:25-34	TJos 8:5 ftnt a
17:23	2En 67:3 ftnt d
19:1	TSol 8:11 ftnt m
19:24	TSol 8:11
19:24	TSol 7:5 ftnt d
19:27	TSol 8:11
19:27f.	TSol 7:5 ftnt d
19:28	SibOr 5.293
19:34	TSol 8:11
19:34f.	TSol 7:5 ftnt d
21:25	SibOr 2.96
22:23	TJob 28:3 ftnt d
23:11	2En 1:7
24:17	VisEzra 3
28:1-6	TJos 6:2 ftnt a
28:26	SibOr 1.360f.

Romans

1:7	2Bar 78:3
1:9	2Bar 86:1
1:17	2Bar 54:17
1:20-21	2Bar 54:18

1:26	SibOr 3.185	2:9	4Ezra 7:15
1:27	ApEl 1:16 ftnt b3	2:10	TJob 37:6 ftnt d
1:29-31	SibOr 1.175	3:6	SibOr 5.262
1:30	VisEzra 50	3:13-15	TAb 12:10 ftnt c
1:32	2En 10:4	3:13-15	TAb 12:14 ftnt g
2:4	TAb 10:14 ftnt g	3:13f.	TAb 13:13 ftnt i
2:5	ApEl 1:19	3:14	4Ezra 7:99
2:5	ApEl 5:24 ftnt u2	4:5	2Bar 83:3
2:14	ApSedr 15:4	5:10f.	SibOr 1.175
2:14-15	2Bar 48:40	6:3	1En 13:10
3:1	2Bar 14:4	6:3	1En 14:3
3:25	TAb 10:14 ftnt g	6:9	TJac 7:19
4:15	2Bar 15:2	6:9-11	TJob 25:1 ftnt a
4:17	2Bar 21:5	6:9f.	SibOr 1.175
5:12	2Bar 17:3	6:9f.	SibOr 3.185
5:12	2Bar 54:15	7:1	TSol 2:3 ftnt e
5:15	SibOr 8.259	7:1	2En 59:1 ftnt a
6:23	2En 30:16	7:29-31	4Ezra 16:41
7:1-6	SibOr 8.300	7:31	TJob 33:4 ftnt h
8:15	ApocEzek Frag 2	8:5	ApZeph A ftnt a
8:18	2Bar 15:8	8:10	SibOr 2.96
8:35	2En 66:6	9:24	3Bar 12:6 (Gk.) ftnt d
8:38	TJob 47:9 ftnt g	9:24	SibOr 2.39f.
9:19	2Bar 3:7	9:25	GkApEzra 6:17 ftnt f
9:22	2Bar 24:2	9:25	2Bar 15:8
9:33	SibOr 8.246	9:25	TBenj 4:1 ftnt a
10:5	2Bar 67:6	11:6	TJob 23:7 ftnt e
10:19	3Bar 16:3	11:7	TNaph 2:5
11:21	2Bar 13:10	13:1	TJob 48:2 ftnt e
11:25	2Bar 23:5	13:1	TJob 38:1 ftnt a
11:26	TBenj 10:11	13:1-3	ApSedr 1:2
11:34	2En 33:4	13:12	TJob 33:8 ftnt l
12:1	SibOr 8.408	14:15	TJob 43:2 ftnt a
12:1	TLevi 3:6	14:25	2Bar 83:3
12:17	ApSedr 7:9	14:26	TJob 47:9 ftnt g
12:19	2En 50:4	15:19	2Bar 21:13
12:19	TGad 6:7	15:20	SibOr 8.314
13:10	ApSedr 1:14	15:21	2Bar 17:3
13:13	SibOr 1.175	15:23	2Bar 14:1a ftnt a
15:33	TDan 5:2	15:24-25	2Bar 73:1
16:15	TJob 51:2 ftnt b	15:29	QuesEzra 32
16:22	TJob 51:4 ftnt f	15:38	ApZeph 10:14
		15:41	2Bar 51:1
1 Corinthians		15:44	ApEl 5:32 ftnt h3
1:3	2Bar 78:3	15:45	2En 42:5 ftnt d
1:17-25	SibOr 8.246	15:45	SibOr 8.259
2:6	SibOr 2.219 ftnt q2	15:47	SibOr 8.445
2:6-8	ApAdam 6:8 ftnt d	15:51	2Bar 49:3

1 Corinthians (cont.)

15:51	2Bar 51:1
15:51	TBenj 10:8
15:51f.	QuesEzra RecB 13
15:52	SibOr 8.239
15:52	4Ezra 6:23
15:52	GkApEzra 4:36
15:52	2Bar 30:2
15:53	2En 8:5 ftnt l
15:55	SibOr 8.415

2 Corinthians

1:2	2Bar 78:3
2:9	TJob 12:1 ftnt a
2:11	TJob 6:4 ftnt c
3:18	ApZeph 5:4 ftnt a
4:6	2En 26:1 ftnt i2
4:17	2Bar 15:8
4:17	2Bar 48:50
5:1-2	2Bar 48:6
5:1-5	3En 18:22 ftnt i2
5:3	2En 22:8 ftnt m
5:3-4	2En 22:8
5:4	4Ezra 14:15
5:14	SibOr 1.371 ftnt g2
6:14	2En 34:1
6:14–7:1	2En 34:1 ftnt a
6:15	TReu 4:7 ftnt c
6:15	SibOr 2.166
6:18	ApZeph 2:9 ftnt i
9:7	2En 61:5
11:3	2En 31:6
11:13-15	TJob 6:4 ftnt c
11:27	2En 66:6
12:1-3	2En 42:3 ftnt c
12:1-4	ApZeph 5:6 ftnt b
12:2	2En 8:1
12:2	2En 42:3
12:2	TLevi 2:7 ftnt d
12:2f.	TJob 39:12 ftnt e
12:2f.	TJob 48:2 ftnt d
12:4	2En 8:1
12:4	2Bar 4:7

Galatians

4:3	TSol 8:2
4:3	TSol 18:2
4:4	2Bar 29:8 ftnt i
4:4	2Bar 40:4
4:6	ApocEzek Frag 2
4:9	TSol 8:2
4:9	TSol 18:2
4:26	4Ezra 10:7
4:26	3En 48A:3 ftnt h
5:7	SibOr 2.39f.
6:7	2En 42:11
6:7f.	TLevi 13:6

Ephesians

1:17	TJob 33:3 ftnt g
1:20	TJob 33:3 ftnt g
1:21	TAdam 4:1 ftnt c
2:2	2En 29:4
2:2	2En 3:1 ftnt e
2:2	TJob 42:4 ftnt c
2:12	ApEl 1:14
2:13	2Bar 42:3 ftnt c
2:14	2Bar 54:5
2:17	2Bar 42:3 ftnt c
2:19	TJob 18:4 ftnt d
4:4	TJud 25:3
4:4-6	2Bar 48:24
4:8	ApEl 1:4
4:8f.	GkApEzra 7:3 ftnt a
4:9	SibOr 1.378
4:18	ApEl 1:13 ftnt q2
4:25	2En 42:12
5:5	TJud 19:1
5:12	2En 34:1
5:18	TJud 14:1
5:18f.	TJob 43:2 ftnt a
5:19	SibOr 8.497
6:5	2En 66:2
6:5	TReu 4:1 ftnt a
6:10	ApEl 4:16 ftnt e2
6:12	TLevi 3:10
6:12	TSol 8:3
6:12	TSol 18:2
6:13-17	TLevi 8:2 ftnt b
6:14	ApEl 4:31 ftnt g3

Philippians

1:23	2Bar 3:7
2:6-8	ApEl 1:6
2:12	2En 66:2
2:15	ApAdam 7:52

Hebrews (cont.)

1:7	4Ezra 8:22
1:7	2En 39:5 ftnt d
3:11	ApEl 2:53 ftnt t3
3:18	ApEl 2:53 ftnt t3
4:1-11	ApEl 2:53 ftnt t3
4:3	2En 53:3
4:3	2Bar 73:1
4:12	2Bar 83:3
5:9-14	TSol 3:5 ftnt b
5:12	1En 61:7
6:13-18	TMos 3:9
7:3	TJob 33:7 ftnt k
7:3	ApAb 17:10 ftnt g
8:1	TJob 33:3 ftnt g
8:1-5	SibOr 4.10
8:2	2Bar 4:3 ftnt b
8:5	TJob 48:2 ftnt e
8:5	2Bar 59:3
8:10	4Ezra 1:29
9:1	TJob 48:2 ftnt e
9:11f.	SibOr 4.10
9:15	TDan 6:2 ftnt a
9:26	TJob 4:6 ftnt b
9:26	TReu 6:8 ftnt c
9:28	TJob 48:2 ftnt e
10:1	TJob 33:7 ftnt k
10:12	TJob 33:7 ftnt k
10:14	TJob 33:7 ftnt k
10:30	2En 50:4
10:32	2En 50:3
10:38	2Bar 54:17
11:3	2En 24:2
11:3	2En 25:1
11:3	2En 48:5
11:3	2Bar 14:17
11:5	2En 1a:1 ftnt d
11:8-16	TJob 18:4 ftnt d
11:9	TAb rec. A 8:6
11:10	TJob 39:12 ftnt f
11:10	4Ezra 10:27
11:12	GkApEzra 2:32
11:13	ApEl 1:13 ftnt t2
11:16	ApEl 1:10 ftnt j
11:38	ApDan 14:9
11:39-40	ApEl 1:13 ftnt t2
12:1	SibOr 2.39f.
12:4-11	2Bar 13:10
12:22-24	TDan 6:2 ftnt a
12:22-24	TJob 48:2 ftnt e
12:28	2En 1a:4 ftnt j
13:2	TJob 23:2 ftnt c
13:2	TAb 2:2 ftnt b
13:9-14	TJob 20:7 ftnt e
13:20f.	TDan 5:2
13:22	2Bar 81:1

James

1:2	2Bar 52:6 ftnt b
1:12	GkApEzra 6:17 ftnt f
1:12	2En 50:3
1:12	2Bar 15:8
1:12	ApEl 1:8
1:12	ApEl 1:14
1:12	TBenj 4:1 ftnt a
1:17	2En 33:4
1:22	ApZeph 10:8
1:23	TJob 33:8 ftnt l
1:27	ApEl 1:2 ftnt f
2:5	ApEl 1:14
2:7	ApAdam 3:18
2:15f.	VisEzra 6
2:23	TAb 1:6 ftnt g
2:23	ApZeph 9:5
2:23	ApAb 9:7
3:7	TJob 3:3 ftnt b
3:9	2En 44:1
4:1	ApEl 1:16
4:2	GkApEzra 1:14 ftnt o
4:4	ApEl 1:2 ftnt f
4:8	ApEl 1:26 ftnt s3
4:14	2Bar 14:10
5:3	2Bar 23:7
5:4	TJob 12:4 ftnt b
5:7	TAb 13:4 ftnt a
5:11	TJob 1:5
5:11	TJob 37:1 ftnt a
5:12	2En 49:1
5:14f.	TAdam 1:7

1 Peter

1:7	4Ezra 16:73
1:12	2En 24:3
2:4	SibOr 1.345-6

2:4	TSol 23:4	3:12	TAb 13:4 ftnt a
2:6	SibOr 8.254	3:13	1En 72:2
2:6-8	SibOr 8.246		
2:6-8	TSol 22:8	*1 John*	
2:7	TSol 23:4	1:5	SibOr Frag 3.34
2:11	ApEl 1:17	1:6-7	SibOr Frag 1.27
2:19	2En 50:3	2:15	ApEl 1:2
2:19	2En 51:3	2:17	TJob 33:4 ftnt h
3:9	ApSedr 7:9	2:20	TSol 4:12
3:14	2En 51:3	2:28	TAb 13:4 ftnt a
3:19	SibOr 1.378	4:12	SibOr 3.17
3:19	SibOr 8.310	4:12	SibOr Frag 1.10
3:20	SibOr 1.205	4:20	ApSedr 1:10
4:2	TAb 12:14 ftnt g	4:21	ApSedr 1:12
4:6	SibOr 8.310	5:16f.	TIss 7:1
4:7	2Bar 23:7		
4:8	ApSedr 1:2	*Jude*	
5:4	2Bar 15:8	5	1En 10:4
5:4	TBenj 4:1 ftnt a	6	1En 10:12
5:4	GkApEzra 6:17 ftnt f	6	2En 7:1
5:7	ApEl 3:1 ftnt a	6	2En 7:1 ftnt d
5:8	ApEl 1:4 ftnt p	6	SibOr 1.98 ftnt f
5:8	ApEl 2:7	6	2Bar 48:9 ftnt b
5:8	TSol 2:3	6-7	TSol 1:13 ftnt p
		7	TNaph 3:4
2 Peter		9	TSol 1:7
1:19	4Ezra 12:43	13	2En 40:13
1:2-4	ApEl 1:13 ftnt t2	13	TSol 16:2
2:4	2En 7:1	13	ApEl 4:11 ftnt u
2:4	2En 7:1 ftnt d	13	TLevi 3:2 ftnt a
2:4	SibOr 1.98 ftnt f	13	2En 11:2 ftnt g
2:4	VisEzra 8 ftnt u	14	1En 1:9
2:4	TLevi 3:2 ftnt a	14	2En 71:32 ftnt o
2:5	SibOr 1.149 ftnt m	15	1En 1:9
3:3	1En 72:2	15	1En 1:9 ftnt y
3:3	TDan 5:4	22	TNaph 3:3
3:5	2En 33:4	23	TNaph 3:3
3:5	2En 47:4		
3:8	ApEl 5:37 ftnt p3	*Revelation*	
3:9	2Bar 21:21	1:1	2Bar 10:3
3:9	2Bar 48:40	1:1	TJob 47:9 ftnt g
3:10	GkApEzra 4:38 ftnt p2	1:1	TJob 1:4 ftnt j
		1:8	2Bar 21:9
3:10	ApEl 1:4 ftnt r	1:8	TIsaac 6:34
3:10-13	ApEl 5:38 ftnt q3	1:9-19	TJob 2:1 ftnt a
3:10f.	TSol 8:2 ftnt a	1:10	2En 33:2 ftnt b
3:12	SibOr 2.199	1:12	ApSedr 2:1

Revelation (cont.)

1:13-15	ApZeph 6:12
1:14	2En 1:5
1:14	SibOr 6.28
1:14	ApAb 11:3
1:16	TSol 8:2 ftnt a
1:16	2En 1:5
1:17	3En 1:7
1:17	4Ezra 10:30
1:19	2En 39:2
1:20	TSol 8:2 ftnt a
2:1	TSol 8:2 ftnt a
2:1	TJob 51:4 ftnt f
2:7	1En 25:5
2:7	2En 8:3
2:7	4Ezra 2:11
2:7	4Ezra 8:52
2:7	2Bar 4:7
2:9	SibOr 7.135
2:9	TJob 3:6 ftnt c
2:10	GkApEzra 6:17 ftnt f
2:10	ApEl 1:8 ftnt b2
2:10	2Bar 15:8
2:10	TBenj 4:1 ftnt a
2:13	TJob 3:6 ftnt c
2:17	2Bar 29:8
2:18	ApZeph 6:13
2:27	SibOr 8.248
3:4	4Ezra 2:40
3:4-5	2En 22:9
3:5	3En 18:24 ftnt l2
3:5	ApZeph 3:8 ftnt g
3:9	SibOr 7.135
3:9	TJob 3:6 ftnt c
3:11	GkApEzra 6:17 ftnt f
3:12	ApEl 1:9
3:18	2En 22:9
3:18	TAb 12:14 ftnt g
4:1	2Bar 10:3
4:1	2Bar 22:2
4:1	2Bar 23:7
4:1-11	TLevi 3:9
4:1f.	2En 20:1
4:2	2En 20:3
4:2-3	1En 14:18
4:4	2En 4:1
4:4	2En 22:9
4:4	3En 18:1 ftnt d
4:4	ApEl 4:10
4:4	TJob 33:1 ftnt a
4:4	ApZeph A ftnt c
4:6	2En 3:3
4:6	2En 1a:4 ftnt i
4:6	2En 27:2 ftnt b
4:7	TNaph 5:6
4:7	ApAb 18:5 ftnt d
4:7	TNaph 5:6 ftnt c
4:8	ApEl 5:2
4:8	2En 22:10 ftnt q
4:10	3En 18:1 ftnt d
5:1	2En 20:3
5:4	2En 1:3 ftnt e
5:8	3Bar 11:8 (Gk.) ftnt g
5:11	ApZeph 4:1f.
6:1f.	SibOr 8.244 ftnt i2
6:4	2Bar 51:11 ftnt d
6:10	SibOr 3.313
6:11	2En 22:9
6:11	4Ezra 2:40
6:11	4Ezra 2:41
6:11	2Bar 23:5
6:11	2En 22:8 ftnt m
6:12	SibOr 2.205
6:12	ApocEzek Frag 2
6:12	ApEl 3:8
6:12-14	SibOr 8.233
6:14	SibOr 3.82
6:14	SibOr 8.413
6:15	ApDan 2:15
6:15f.	3En 32:2 ftnt d
6:16	ApEl 2:34
6:17	ApZeph 12:6
7:1	4Ezra 2:40
7:3	ApEl 1:9
7:5-8	ApDan 8:2 ftnt b
7:9	2En 22:9
7:9	4Ezra 2:42
7:9	2En 22:8 ftnt m
7:11	2Bar 51:11 ftnt d
7:13	2En 22:8 ftnt m
7:13	2En 22:9
7:13	ApEl 5:6 ftnt p
7:14	2En 22:8 ftnt m
7:14	2En 22:9
7:14	SibOr 14.302 ftnt e2
7:16	ApEl 5:6

7:16	ApEl 1:9 ftnt f2
8:3	3Bar 11:8 (Gk.) ftnt g
8:10	SibOr 5.155
9:1	2En 42:1
9:1	SibOr 5.155
9:2	4Ezra 7:36
9:6	SibOr 2.307
9:6	SibOr 8.353
9:6	ApEl 2:5
9:6	ApEl 2:32
9:6	ApDan 12:3
9:8	ApZeph 6:8 ftnt b
9:13-18	SibOr 5.93f.
9:14	TSol 17:4
9:15	SibOr 3.544
9:15	SibOr 5.103
9:17	2En 1:5
9:18	SibOr 3.544
9:18	SibOr 5.103
10:6	TJob 2:4 ftnt c
11:1f.	ApEl 4:7 ftnt m
11:3	ApEl 3:1 ftnt a
11:3-13	ApDan 14:2 ftnt b
11:7-11	ApEl 4:13 ftnt w
11:8	SibOr 6.21
11:8	ApEl 4:13
11:12	ApEl 4:19 ftnt g2
11:15	2En 1:5
11:16	TJob 33:1 ftnt a
11:18	ApEl 5:4 ftnt m
12:1	TNaph 5:1
12:1-3	2Bar 25:4
12:1-6	2En 72:3 ftnt c
12:1-17	TSol 12:1
12:1-17	TAsh 7:3 ftnt a
12:1–ch. 13	SibOr 8.88 ftnt m
12:3	SibOr 8.88
12:4	SibOr 1.314
12:5	SibOr 8.196
12:5	SibOr 8.248
12:6	ApAdam 7:9
12:7	TSol 1:7
12:7	SibOr 5.514 ftnt j4
12:7	TAb 1:4 ftnt b
12:7	TLevi 5:6 ftnt d
12:9	TBenj 3:7 ftnt b
12:11	TJud 25:4
12:14	ApEl 3:1 ftnt a
12:14	TNaph 5:6 ftnt b
12:15	ApEl 1:4 ftnt r
13:1	SibOr 8.88
13:1	4Ezra 11:1
13:5	ApEl 3:1 ftnt a
13:8	ApZeph 3:8 ftnt g
13:13	ApEl 3:6 ftnt m
13:16	TSol 17:4
13:17	TSol 17:4
13:18	ApDan 9:25 ftnt d2
13:18	SibOr 1.141
14:1	ApEl 1:9
14:1	TSol 17:4
14:4	VisEzra 10
14:7	TJob 2:4 ftnt c
14:8	SibOr Frag 3.39
14:8	4Ezra 15:47
14:8	SibOr 5.143 ftnt i2
14:15	SibOr 1.387
14:20	4Ezra 15:36
14:20	ApDan 4:8
15:1	2Bar 27:4
15:1	3Bar 4:1 (Gk.) ftnt a
15:2	2En 3:3
15:3	3Bar 4:1 (Gk.) ftnt a
16:5	2En 19:4
16:5	SibOr 7.35
16:7	ApEl 5:24 ftnt u2
16:16	4Ezra 13:34
16:17f.	ApDan 3:7
16:19	SibOr 5.143 ftnt i2
17:1f.	SibOr 2.18
17:1f.	SibOr 8.194
17:4f.	4Ezra 15:47
17:9	SibOr 11.113
17:9	SibOr 13.45
17:9	ApDan 7:5
17:11	SibOr 4.138
17:16	SibOr 8.96f.
17:16	SibOr 8.142 ftnt t
17:18	ApDan 7:5
18:1f.	SibOr 3.302
18:1f.	SibOr 5.162
18:1f.	SibOr 14.208f.
18:1f.	TJob 25:1 ftnt a
18:2	SibOr 5.143 ftnt i2
18:7	SibOr 5.169

Revelation (cont.)

18:7	SibOr 5.173
18:7	ApDan 7:10 ftnt d
18:7-8	SibOr 3.77
18:7f.	SibOr 11.290 ftnt j3
18:7f.	4Ezra 15:49
18:10	ApDan 7:2
18:11	ApEl 2:31
18:13	TJob 32:10 ftnt m
18:16	ApDan 7:2
18:16	ApDan 7:10 ftnt d
18:17-19	ApDan 7:13
18:19	TJob 28:3 ftnt d
18:19	ApDan 7:2
18:21	SibOr 5.143 ftnt i2
18:22	SibOr 5.143 ftnt i2
18:22	SibOr 8.115
19:2	ApEl 5:24 ftnt u2
19:4	2En 20:3
19:9	3En 48A:10 ftnt x
19:9f.	TJob 23:2 ftnt c
19:10	ApZeph 6:15
19:10	2En 1:7 ftnt u
19:12	2En 1:5
19:12	SibOr 6.28
19:12	ApZeph A
19:15	SibOr 8.248
19:15	3En 32:1 ftnt c
19:19	4Ezra 13:34
19:20	2En 10:2
19:20	SibOr 2.292 ftnt x2
19:20	SibOr 8.102
19:20	ApZeph 6:2
20:1	2En 42:1
20:2	TJud 25:3
20:2	TBenj 3:7 ftnt b
20:2	TAsh 7:3 ftnt a
20:2-3	SibOr 8.197
20:3	ApEl 5:35 ftnt m3
20:4	ApEl 1:9
20:4	ApEl 5:39
20:4	TJud 25:4
20:4	TJob 33:1 ftnt a
20:6	ApEl 5:37 ftnt p3
20:7-10	SibOr 3.319
20:8	3En 45:5 ftnt u
20:10	1En 10:13
20:10	SibOr 8.102
20:10-15	2En 10:2
20:11	3En 28:8
20:12	3En 18:24 ftnt l2
20:12	4Ezra 6:20
20:12	2Bar 24:1
20:14	1En 10:13
20:14	TJud 25:3
20:14	ApEl 5:38 ftnt r3
20:14f.	SibOr 2.292 ftnt x2
20:15	1En 10:13
21:1	1En 72:3
21:1	SibOr 5.157 ftnt n2
21:1	SibOr 5.447
21:1	ApEl 5:38
21:2	3En 48A:3 ftnt h
21:2	TJob 18:4 ftnt d
21:3	2En 20:3
21:4	2En 65:9
21:4	2Bar 73:2
21:4	2Bar 73:3
21:4	ApEl 5:38 ftnt r3
21:5	2Bar 73:1 ftnt a
21:5–22:5	TLevi 5:1
21:8	2En 10:2
21:8	2En 10:5
21:8	SibOr 2.255f.
21:8	SibOr 8.102
21:9-21	4Ezra 10:27
21:10	TNaph 5:2 ftnt a
21:18	VisEzra 57 ftnt z5
21:22	SibOr 5.423 ftnt a4
21:23	4Ezra 2:35
22:2	1En 25:5
22:2	2En 8:2
22:2	4Ezra 2:11
22:2	4Ezra 2:19
22:2	4Ezra 8:52
22:2	TLevi 9:12 ftnt d
22:2	TLevi 18:11
22:4	4Ezra 7:98
22:4	TLevi 18:11
22:5	4Ezra 2:35
22:6	TJob 1:4 ftnt j
22:8	ApZeph B
22:8f.	ApZeph 6:15
22:12	4Ezra 7:99

OLD TESTAMENT

Genesis
1:1   PrMan 2
1:1f.   HelSynPr 3:1
1:1f.   HelSynPr 12:18
1:1f.   HelSynPr 15:3
1:1f.–ch. 2   LAE Apoc 42:3 ftnt b
1:1–2:4a   OdesSol 16:7 ftnt d
1:2   PrMan 3 ftnt h
1:2 (LXX)   JosAsen 12:1 ftnt d
1:2 (LXX)   JosAsen 12:2 ftnt e
1:3-5   Aristob Frag 5:9
1:3 (LXX)   Aristob Frag 4:3
1:5   HelSynPr 3:7
1:6 (LXX)   Aristob Frag 4:3
1:6 (LXX)   JosAsen 12:2 ftnt h
1:6   HelSynPr 3:2
1:6   HelSynPr 3:8
1:6-10   PrMan 3
1:7   Jub 2:4
1:9   LAB 15:6
1:9   HelSynPr 3:8
1:9 (LXX)   Aristob Frag 4:3
1:11f.   LAB 60:2
1:14   HelSynPr 3:14
1:14 (LXX)   Aristob Frag 4:3
1:14-18   Aristob Frag 5:12
1:14-19   Jub 2:8
1:14-19   HelSynPr 3:6
1:16   HelSynPr 12:20
1:16-18   OdesSol 16:16
1:20 (LXX)   Aristob Frag 4:3
1:20-23   Jub 2:11
1:24 (LXX)   Aristob Frag 4:3

1:24-28   Jub 2:13
1:26   LAE Vita 14:1
1:26   LAE Apoc 10:3
1:26   HelSynPr 3:19
1:26   HelSynPr 12:36
1:26f.   Ps-Phoc 106 ftnt h
1:27   LAE Vita 12:2
1:28   Ps-Phoc 176 ftnt b
1:28   JosAsen 12:6 ftnt k
1:28   LAE Apoc 10:3
1:29   LAE Vita 22:2
1:29   LAE Apoc 29:6
2:1   PrMan 2
2:2   LAE Vita 51:3
2:2   OdesSol 16:12
2:2   Aristob Frag 5:11
2:2   HelSynPr 5:2
2:2   FrgsPoetWrks 1
                   ftnt e
2:2f.   Aristob Frag 5:9
2:2f.   Aristob Frag 5:14
2:7   JosAsen 12:1 ftnt c
2:7   JosAsen 15:5 ftnt i
2:7   JosAsen 19:11 ftnt m
2:7   LAE Vita 12:2
2:7   LAE Apoc 40:5
2:8   LAE Vita 19:3 ftnt a
2:8   HelSynPr 12:41
2:9   JosAsen 4:2 ftnt d
2:10   JosAsen 24:20 ftnt z
2:11   LAB 26:1 ftnt a
2:11f.   LAB 25:11
2:13   LAE Vita 6:3 ftnt b
2:13   Jub 8:15

2:14	LAE Vita 6:1	3:23	Jub 3:32
2:15-17	HelSynPr 12:44	3:23 (LXX)	JosAsen 16:14 ftnt n
2:16-17	LAE Apoc 7:1	3:24	LAE Apoc 28:3
2:17	JosAsen 18:9 ftnt v	4:1	JosAsen 21:1 ftnt a
2:17	LAE Apoc 17:5	4:1	LAE Vita 21:3
2:19f.	Jub 3:1f.	4:1f.	HelSynPr 6:4
2:21	LAE Apoc 29:10	4:1f.	HelSynPr 12:53
2:21f.	LAB 32:15	4:1-16	LAB 16:2
2:22	4Mac 18:8	4:1-14	Jub 4:1f.
2:23	LAE Vita 3:2	4:2	LAE Vita 23:4
2:24	Ps-Phoc 176 ftnt b	4:5	LAE Apoc 3:2
2:25	Jub 3:16	4:5f.	JosAsen 13:9 ftnt h
3:1	LAE Apoc 16:2	4:8	4Mac 18:10
3:1-7	LAE Vita 16:3	4:9	LAE Vita 23:4
3:1-7	LAE Apoc 7:2	4:10-11	LAE Apoc 40:4
3:1-7	4Mac 18:8	4:12	LAB 2:1 ftnt a
3:1-19	Jub 3:17f.	4:12-16	LAB 2:1
3:1f.	HelSynPr 12:46	4:14	LAB 2:1 ftnt a
3:1f.	PssSol 4:9 ftnt I	4:16	LAB 2:1 ftnt a
3:1f.	EzekTrag 242-243	4:17	Jub 4:7f.
3:3	JosAsen 18:9 ftnt v	4:17	LAB 2:2
3:3	LAE Apoc 17:5	4:17	LAB 2:3
3:5	LAE Apoc 18:3	4:18	LAB 2:5
3:6	LAE Vita 26:2	4:18	LAB 2:5 ftnt c
3:6	LAE Apoc 18:6	4:18	LAB 2:5 ftnt d
3:7	LAE Apoc 20:4	4:19	LAB 2:6
3:7	LAE Apoc 20:5	4:20f.	LAB 2:7
3:7	LAE Apoc 20:1	4:21	LAB 2:8
3:8-12	LAE Apoc 8:1	4:22	LAB 2:9
3:9	LAE Apoc 23:1	4:22	LAB 2:9 ftnt f
3:10	LAE Apoc 23:2	4:23f.	LAB 2:10
3:11	LAE Apoc 23:3	4:25	LAE Apoc 3:2
3:13	LAE Apoc 23:5	4:25	LAE Apoc 38:4
3:14	LAE Apoc 26:1	4:25	LAE Apoc 4:1 ftnt a
3:14	LAE Apoc 26:2	4:25f.	Jub 4:7f.
3:14-15	LAE Apoc 26:1	4:25f.	HelSynPr 12:55
3:15	LAE Apoc 26:4	5:3	LAE Vita 23:5
3:15 (LXX)	LAE Apoc 26:4 ftnt e	5:3	LAE Apoc 12:2 ftnt a
3:16	LAE Apoc 25:1	5:4	LAE Apoc 5:1
3:17-19	LAE Apoc 24:1	5:4	LAB 1:2
3:17-19	HelSynPr 12:48	5:4	LAB 1:2 ftnt c
3:18	LAE Apoc 24:2	5:5	LAE Vita 30:1
3:18	LAB 37:3	5:6	LAB 1:5 ftnt f
3:19	LAE Apoc 24:2	5:6f.	LAB 1:5
3:19	LAE Apoc 41:2	5:6-15	Jub 4:7f.
3:19	Ps-Phoc 107	5:7	LAB 1:5 ftnt g
3:21, 23	Jub 3:26f.	5:9	LAB 1:7 ftnt i
3:22-24	LAE Vita 1:1	5:9f.	LAB 1:7

Genesis (cont.)

5:10	LAB 1:7 ftnt j
5:12	LAB 1:9 ftnt k
5:12-17	LAB 1:9 ftnt l
5:12f.	LAB 1:9
5:13	LAB 1:9 ftnt m
5:15	LAB 1:11 ftnt n
5:15f.	LAB 1:11
5:16	LAB 1:11 ftnt o
5:18	LAB 1:13 ftnt q
5:18f.	LAB 1:13
5:18-24	Jub 4:16f.
5:21	Ps-Eup (PrEv 9.17.9)
5:21	LAB 1:15 ftnt r
5:21f.	LAB 1:15
5:21-24	LAE Vita 51:9
5:22	LAB 1:15 ftnt s
5:24	LAB 1:16
5:24	HelSynPr 12:55
5:25	LAB 1:18 ftnt u
5:25f.	LAB 1:18
5:25-29	Jub 4:27f.
5:28	LAB 1:20 ftnt v
5:28f.	LAB 1:20
5:29	LAB 1:20 ftnt w
5:30	LAB 1:21
5:30	LAB 1:21 ftnt x
5:32	LAB 1:22
5:32	Jub 4:33
5:32	LAB 1:22 ftnt z
6:1f.	LAB 3:1
6:1-5	Jub 5:1f.
6:1–ch. 9	HelSynPr 12:58
6:2	LAB 3:1 ftnt a
6:3	LAB 3:2
6:3	LAB 3:2 ftnt b
6:3	LAB 3:2 ftnt c
6:3	LAB 9:8
6:3	LAB 48:1
6:4-7	3Mac 2:4
6:5	LAB 3:3
6:5–8:22	4Mac 15:31
6:7	LAB 3:3
6:7-13	Jub 5:3f.
6:8f.	LAB 3:4
6:11	JosAsen 26:3 ftnt g
6:13-15	LAB 3:4
6:14	LAB 3:4 ftnt d

6:14–8:19	Jub 5:20f.
6:18	LAB 3:4
6:19-21	LAB 3:4
7:1f.	3Mac 2:4
7:1f.	HelSynPr 8:3
7:2-4	LAB 3:4
7:5	LAB 3:5
7:7	LAB 3:5
7:10-12	LAB 3:5
7:11	LAB 3:5 ftnt e
7:11 (LXX)	Dem Frag 2:18 ftnt d
7:23–8:1	LAB 3:7
8:7-12	4Bar 7:8
8:14	LAB 3:8 ftnt g
8:14-21	LAB 3:8
8:18	LAB 3:8 ftnt h
8:20	Jub 6:1f.
8:20-22	HelSynPr 6:4
8:21	LAB 3:9
8:21	LAB 3:8 ftnt i
8:21	LAB 3:9 ftnt j
8:22	LAB 3:9
8:21–9:17	Jub 6:4f.
9:1	LAB 3:11
9:2	JosAsen 9:1 ftnt a
9:3f.	LAB 3:11
9:6	SyrMen 18-19
9:6f.	LAB 3:11
9:8f.	LAB 3:11
9:11	LAB 3:11
9:12	LAB 3:12
9:12	LAB 3:12 ftnt n
9:13	LAB 19:11
9:14	LAB 3:12
9:14	LAB 3:12 ftnt o
9:15	LAB 19:11
9:16	LAB 3:12
9:18	LAB 4:1
9:20	Jub 7:1f.
9:21-27	Jub 7:7f.
9:28	Jub 10:15
9:28f.	LAB 5:8
10:1f.	Jub 9:1f.
10:1f.	Ps-Eup (PrEv 9.17.9) ftnt u
10:1f. (LXX)	JosAsen 2:11 ftnt q
10:1–ch. 11	Ps-Eup (PrEv 9.17.3)
10:2	LAB 4:2 ftnt a

10:2-4	LAB 4:2	11:21	LAB 4:12
10:2-4	LAB 5:4	11:22	Jub 11:7f.
10:2-5	Jub 8:25f.	11:22f.	LAB 4:13
10:4	Jub 24:29	11:23	LAB 4:13 ftnt p2
10:5	LAB 4:3	11:24	Jub 11:9f.
10:6	Ps-Eup (PrEv 9.17.9)	11:24f.	LAB 4:14
	ftnt u	11:26	Jub 11:14f.
10:6	EzekTrag 65 ftnt y	11:26f.	LAB 4:15
10:6f.	LAB 4:6	11:29	Jub 12:9f.
10:6f.	LAB 5:5	11:29	LAB 23:4
10:6-20	Jub 8:22f.	11:31	Jub 12:15f.
10:7	LAB 4:6 ftnt y	11:31	Ps-Eup (PrEv 9.17.3)
10:8f.	LAB 4:7	12:1-3	Jub 12:22f.
10:13	LAB 4:7 ftnt d2	12:1-4	Ps-Eup (PrEv 9.17.4)
10:13f.	LAB 4:7	12:1f.	HelSynPr 12:62
10:15-18	LAB 4:6	12:2	Jub 20:10
10:15-18	LAB 4:6 ftnt b2	12:4-8	Jub 13:1f.
10:19	LAB 4:8	12:4f.	LAB 8:1
10:19	Ps-Eup (PrEv 9.17.4)	12:5	Ps-Eup (PrEv 9.17.4)
	ftnt j	12:5	Ps-Eup (PrEv 9.18.2)
10:22	LAB 5:6	12:7	LAB 10:2
10:22	LivPro 3:3	12:7	LAB 12:4
10:22-25	LAB 4:9	12:7	LAB 23:5
10:24f.	Jub 8:5f.	12:7	HelSynPr 6:5
10:26	LAB 6:3 ftnt c	12:9–13:2	Jub 13:10f.
10:26-29	LAB 4:10	12:10	Ps-Eup (PrEv 9.17.6)
10:26-31	Jub 8:12f.	12:10	Ps-Eup (PrEv 9.18.2)
10:28f.	LAB 6:3 ftnt c	12:10	Art Frag 1 (PrEv
10:29	LAB 6:3 ftnt c		9.18.1)
10:31f.	LAB 4:17	12:11-15	Ps-Eup (PrEv 9.17.6)
10:32	LAE Vita 24:4	12:14	JosAsen 23:1 ftnt b
11:1-9	Jub 10:18f.	12:17-19	Ps-Eup (PrEv 9.17.7)
11:1-26 (LXX)	Dem Frag 2:18 ftnt d	13:3-17	Jub 13:15f.
11:2-4	LAB 6:1	13:11-13	LAB 8:2
11:3	LAB 6:2	13:12	LAB 8:1
11:4	LAB 7:1	13:14f.	Eup 30:3 ftnt h
11:5f.	LAB 7:2	13:15	LAB 8:3
11:6	LAB 12:3	13:16	HelSynPr 2:16
11:7	LAB 7:3	13:16	Jub 19:22
11:7	LAB 7:5	14:1-12	Ps-Eup (PrEv 9.17.4)
11:7	LAB 32:1	14:1-14	Jub 13:22f.
11:8f.	LAB 7:5	14:13	Art Frag 1 (PrEv
11:9	LAB 7:5 ftnt d		9.18.1) ftnt b
11:10	LivPro 3:3	14:13-16	Ps-Eup (PrEv 9.17.4)
11:10	Dem Frag 2:18 ftnt d	14:16	Ps-Eup (PrEv 9.17.4)
11:17-20	LAB 4:10		ftnt l
11:18	Jub 10:18f.	14:17 (LXX)	FrgsPoetWrks 4
11:20	Jub 11:1f.		ftnt k

Genesis (cont.)

14:18	HelSynPr 12:63
14:18	Ps-Eup (PrEv 9.17.6) ftnt o
14:18-20	Ps-Eup (PrEv 9.17.4)
14:19	Jub 22:11
14:19 (LXX)	JosAsen 8:2 ftnt f
14:19-20	JosAsen 3:3 ftnt f
14:20	Jub 13:25f.
14:20b	Ps-Eup (PrEv 9.17.6) ftnt o
14:21-24	Jub 13:28f.
14:21-24	Ps-Eup (PrEv 9.17.4)
15:1-6	PhEPoet Frags 1-2 ftnt f
15:1-17	Jub 14:1f.
15:2-5	LAB 23:5
15:7	Jub 22:27
15:9f.	LAB 23:6
15:12	LAB 23:6
15:13	LAB 9:3
15:13	Dem Frag 2:16 ftnt d
15:13f.	LAB 15:5
15:13f.	LadJac 5:16
15:13f.	Jub 48:8
15:15	4Mac 5:37
15:17	LAB 23:6
15:17-21	Jub 14:17f.
15:18	PrJac 1:5
15:18	Theod Frag 6 ftnt e
16:1	LAB 8:1
16:1-4	Jub 14:21f.
16:5	JosAsen 28:7 ftnt h
16:10	LAB 49:6
16:14	Jub 24:1
16:15	Jub 14:21f.
16:15	LAB 8:1
17:1	LAB 8:3
17:1-16	Jub 15:1f.
17:5	JosAsen 15:7 ftnt l
17:5	LAB 8:3
17:5	PrJos Frag A ftnt a
17:7	HelSynPr 2:18
17:9-27	Theod Frag 5
17:15	JosAsen 15:7 ftnt l
17:15	LAB 8:3
17:15	PrJos Frag A ftnt a
17:17-22	Jub 15:17f.
17:19	HelSynPr 12:64
17:23-27	Jub 15:23f.
18:1-5	JosAsen 15:14 ftnt f2
18:1-15	Jub 16:1f.
18:4	JosAsen 7:1 ftnt b
18:16–19:20	Jub 16:5f.
18:17	LAB 18:5
18:25	JosAsen 23:11 ftnt w
18:30	LAB 35:6
19:1f.	HelSynPr 12:61
19:5	LAB 45:3
19:9	LAB 45:3
19:10f.	LAB 45:2
19:24	3Mac 2:5
19:24	HelSynPr 8:3
19:24	Jub 16:5
19:30-38	Jub 16:7f.
20:1–21:7	Jub 16:10f.
20:8	JosAsen 19:6 ftnt e
20:12	Jub 12:9
21:1	LAB 18:5 ftnt f
21:1-3	PhEPoet Frags 1-2 ftnt k
21:2f.	LAB 8:3
21:5	Dem Frag 2:16 ftnt a
21:5	Dem Frag 3:2 ftnt d
21:8	Jub 16:20f.
21:8	Jub 17:1f.
21:9-21	Jub 17:4f.
21:10	JosAsen 24:8 ftnt k
21:12	Jub 16:17
22:1	Jub 17:15f.
22:1f.	Dem Frag 1
22:1f.	LAB 40:2
22:1f.	4Mac 7:15
22:1f.	4Mac 13:12
22:1f.	4Mac 18:11
22:1-10	LAB 32:2
22:1-19	Jub 18:1f.
22:3-6	PhEPoet Frags 1-2 ftnt g
22:3-8	PhEPoet Frags 1-2 ftnt f
22:6	PhEPoet Frags 1-2 ftnt i
22:9	PhEPoet Frags 1-2 ftnt b
22:9-18	LAB 32:4

22:10	4Mac 16:20	26:19	JosAsen 2:12 ftnt r
22:10	PhEPoet Frags 1-2 ftnt m	26:20	Theod Frag 2 ftnt a
		26:23-25	HelSynPr 6:5
22:11-13	PhEPoet Frags 1-2 ftnt o	26:34	LAB 8:5
		26:35	Jub 25:1
22:16	PhEPoet Frags 1-2 ftnt j	27:1-40	Jub 26:1f.
		27:2	Jub 21:1
22:17	LAB 14:2	27:18f.	JosAsen 14:6 ftnt j
22:17	LAB 18:5	27:29	Jub 22:11
22:17	HelSynPr 2:16	27:29	Jub 25:22
23:1-20	Jub 19:1f.	27:41	Jub 26:35f.
23:9	LivPro 3:4	27:41-45	Theod Frag 3
24:1–25:3	Jub 19:10f.	27:41–28:5	Dem Frag 2:1
24:3	JosAsen 7:5 ftnt k	27:41b-45	LadJac 1:3 ftnt a
25:1-3 (LXX)	Dem Frag 3:1 ftnt e	27:42–28:5	Jub 27:1f.
25:1-3	Dem Frag 3:2 ftnt c	27:45–28:9	LadJac 1:3 ftnt a
25:1-3	Dem Frag 3:3 ftnt b	27:46	Jub 25:1
25:1-4 (LXX)	Dem Frag 3:1	28:1	Jub 22:20
25:1-6	ClMal 240	28:1	Jub 25:1
25:2	Dem Frag 3:2 ftnt c	28:1	JosAsen 7:5 ftnt k
25:2	Dem Frag 3:3 ftnt c	28:1f.	Jub 25:3
25:2	Jub 16:16	28:1f.	HelSynPr 2:19 ftnt b
25:3f.	ClMal 241	28:6	JosAsen 7:5 ftnt k
25:4	Dem Frag 3:3 ftnt c	28:6	Theod Frag 3
25:5, 7	Jub 21:1f.	28:9	Jub 29:18
25:5f.	Jub 20:1f.	28:9	LAB 8:5
25:6	Dem Frag 3:3 ftnt d	28:10-22	Jub 27:19f.
25:6	EzekTrag 60 ftnt x	28:10-27	PrJos Frag A
25:8	Jub 23:8	28:11-12a	LadJac 1:1
25:8f.	Jub 23:1f.	28:12b	LadJac 1:7
25:11	Jub 24:1f.	28:13	Aristob Frag 2:9
25:12	LAB 8:1	28:13f.	LadJac 1:9
25:13-15	Jub 20:1	28:15	HelSynPr 2:20
25:19-26	Dem Frag 3:2 ftnt a	28:17-19	LadJac 2:3
25:20	Dem Frag 3:2 ftnt d	28:22	Jub 32:5
25:24-28	Jub 19:10f.	29:1-25	Jub 28:1f.
25:16	LAB 8:1	29:13-30	Theod Frag 3
25:20	LAB 32:5 ftnt h	29:26f.	Jub 28:6f.
25:20-26	LAB 8:4	29:28–30:24	Jub 28:9f.
25:21	LAB 32:5	29:31–30:24	Dem Frag 2:3
25:26	Dem Frag 2:16 ftnt b	29:31–30:24	LAB 8:6
25:26	LAB 32:5 ftnt h	29:31–30:24	Dem Frag 2:8 ftnt b
25:27-34	Jub 24:1f.	29:34	Dem Frag 3:2 ftnt a
25:28	Jub 19:15f.	30:1-8	Dem Frag 2:3 ftnt c
26:1	Jub 24:2	30:1-13	JosAsen 22:11 ftnt m
26:1-5	Jub 24:8f.	30:4f.	JosAsen 21:9 ftnt r
26:11	Jub 24:13	30:10	JosAsen 21:9 ftnt r
26:12-33	Jub 24:14f.	30:14	Dem Frag 2:4

Genesis (cont.)

30:21	Dem Frag 2:5 ftnt a
30:25	Dem Frag 2:3 ftnt b
30:25–31:1	Jub 28:25f.
30:37-39	LAB 17:3
31:2-21	Jub 29:1f.
31:11-13	JosAsen 14:6 ftnt j
31:17	PrJos Frag A
31:21	Theod Frag 3
31:21-55	Jub 29:5f.
31:38	Dem Frag 2:6
31:40	JosAsen 18:4 ftnt f
31:41	Dem Frag 2:6 ftnt a
32:22	Jub 29:13
32:24-27	LAB 18:6
32:24-28	Dem Frag 2:10 ftnt b
32:24-28	PrJos Frag A
32:24-31	PrJos Frag A ftnt k
32:24-32	Dem Frag 2:7
32:25-33	JosAsen 22:7 ftnt j
32:27f.	PrJos Frag A
32:29	JosAsen 15:7 ftnt l
32:30	JosAsen 15:12 ftnt c2
32:30	OdesSol 25:4 ftnt e
33:17–34:31	Jub 30:1f.
33:18	PrJos Frag A
33:18	Dem Frag 2:8
33:18	LAB 8:7
33:18 (LXX)	Dem Frag 2:8 ftnt a
33:18 (LXX)	Theod Frag 3 ftnt a
33:18-20	Theod Frag 1 ftnt g
33:18-20	Theod Frag 2
33:18-20	Theod Frag 4
33:19	Theod Frag 4 ftnt b
34:1f.	JosAsen 23:2 ftnt f
34:1f.	Dem Frag 2:9
34:1f.	4Mac 2:19
34:1f.	Theod Frag 1 ftnt c
34:1f.	Theod Frag 4 ftnt a
34:1f.	Theod Frag 6 ftnt a
34:1f.	Theod Frag 7 ftnt a
34:1-12	Theod Frag 4
34:2	LAB 8:7
34:2 (LXX)	LAB 8:7 ftnt g
34:4	JosAsen 1:7 ftnt s
34:7	Jub 30:7
34:13	Theod Frag 6 ftnt b
34:13-17	Theod Frag 4

34:14	Jub 30:12
34:14-17	Theod Frag 4 ftnt e
34:18-24	Theod Frag 6
34:25	Theod Frag 6
34:25f.	Theod Frag 8
34:25f.	LAB 8:7
34:26	JosAsen 26:5 ftnt i
34:26-29	Theod Frag 8
34:25-31	JosAsen 22:11 ftnt m
34:25-31	JosAsen 23:7 ftnt o
34:26-31	Jub 30:24f.
35:1-4	Jub 31:1f.
35:1-27	Dem Frag 2:10
35:1f.	HelSynPr 6:5
35:4	LAB 25:10 ftnt k
35:5	Jub 30:24f.
35:6 (LXX)	Dem Frag 2:10 ftnt a
35:7	Jub 31:3f.
35:8	Jub 32:30
35:8	LivPro 10:8
35:9	PrJos Frag A
35:9f.	HelSynPr 13:8
35:10	PrJos Frag A
35:10	Dem Frag 2:10 ftnt b
35:16	Dem Frag 2:10 ftnt c
35:16-19	Dem Frag 2:10 ftnt d
35:16-20	Jub 32:33f.
35:18	LAB 8:6
35:21f.	Jub 33:1f.
35:22-27	Jub 33:21f.
35:23	Dem Frag 2:14 ftnt d
35:23-26	LAB 8:6
35:27	Dem Frag 2:11 ftnt a
35:27	Dem Frag 2:11 ftnt b
35:28f.	Dem Frag 2:11 ftnt f
35:29	Jub 36:18
36:2	LAB 8:5
36:4	LAB 8:5
36:5	LAB 8:5
36:6	Jub 29:18
36:8	Jub 29:18
36:10	ArisEx (PrEv 9.25.1)
36:11	LAB 8:5
36:13	LAB 8:5
36:13	ArisEx (PrEv 9.25.1)
36:14	LAB 8:5
36:15	LivPro 10:10
36:18	LAB 8:5

36:31-35	ArisEx (AddJob) c	41:14-32	PhEPoet Frag 3 ftnt e
36:31-39	Jub 38:15f.	41:34	JosAsen 3:1 ftnt b
36:33	LAB 8:8 ftnt h	41:36	JosAsen 26:3 ftnt g
36:33	ArisEx (PrEv 9.25.3)	41:38	JosAsen 4:7 ftnt p
36:33	ArisEx (AddJob) b	41:39	JosAsen 4:7 ftnt p
36:33	ArisEx (AddJob) c	41:39	HistJos A Recto 4
36:42	LivPro 10:10	41:39-41	PhEPoet Frag 3 ftnt f
37:1	LAB 8:7	41:39-45	HistJos A Recto 27
37:1	LAB 8:9	41:39-49	Jub 40:6f.
37:1f.	JosAsen 22:11 ftnt m	41:41	JosAsen 4:7 ftnt k
37:1f.	Jub 39:1f.	41:41	Art Frag 2 (PrEv
37:2	Dem Frag 2:9 ftnt a		9.23.2)
37:2	Dem Frag 2:11 ftnt c	41:42	JosAsen 5:5 ftnt k
37:4	LAB 8:9	41:42	JosAsen 5:5 ftnt l
37:5-20	Art Frag 2 (PrEv	41:43	Jub 40:7
	9.23:1)	41:43	JosAsen 5:4 ftnt f
37:9	EzekTrag 67 ftnt z	41:43	LAB 8:10
37:12	Jub 34:1f.	41:43-44	HistJos A Recto 8
37:13-35	Jub 34:10f.	41:44	Ah 122
37:25	JosAsen 14:9 ftnt o	41:44	JosAsen 4:7 ftnt k
37:25-28	JosAsen 24:9 ftnt l	41:45	JosAsen 1:2 ftnt e
37:26 (LXX)	LAB 8:9 ftnt j	41:45	JosAsen 1:3 ftnt i
37:36	JosAsen 1:3 ftnt i	41:45	JosAsen 1:5 ftnt l
37:36	LAB 8:9	41:45	JosAsen 6:6 ftnt r
38:1-30	Jub 41:1f.	41:45	JosAsen 15:7 ftnt l
38:2	Jub 34:20f.	41:45	Art Frag 2 (PrEv
38:6f.	Jub 41:1		9.23.3)
38:18	LAB 9:5 ftnt i	41:45	Dem Frag 2:12 ftnt a
38:24	Jub 20:4	41:45 (LXX)	Art Frag 3 (PrEv
38:24f.	LAB 9:5		9.27.1)
38:25	LAB 9:5 ftnt i	41:45-49	Dem Frag 2:12 ftnt b
39:1	JosAsen 1:3 ftnt i	41:46	Dem Frag 2:11 ftnt d
39:1	LAB 8:9	41:47	JosAsen 3:1 ftnt b
39:1f.	JosAsen 4:7 ftnt p	41:47-49	Art Frag 2 (PrEv
39:1f.	LAB 43:5		9.23.4)
39:1-40:23	Jub 39:1f.	41:48-49	HistJos A Recto 17
39:1-ch. 41	JosAsen 4:10 ftnt x	41:49	JosAsen 1:2 ftnt f
39:7	JosAsen 6:4 ftnt l	41:50	JosAsen 1:2 ftnt e
39:7-10	JosAsen 7:2 ftnt e	41:50	JosAsen 1:3 ftnt i
39:7-12	4Mac 2:3	41:50	JosAsen 1:5 ftnt l
39:7-23	4Mac 18:11	41:50	Art Frag 2 (PrEv
39:9	JosAsen 23:11 ftnt y		9.23.3)
39:19 (LXX)	JosAsen 23:9 ftnt r	41:50-52	JosAsen 21:9 ftnt r
39:20	JosAsen 4:10 ftnt x	41:50-52	Dem Frag 2:12 ftnt b
41:1	LAB 8:10	41:53	Jub 41:22
41:1-38	Jub 40:1f.	41:53-56	Jub 42:1f.
41:1f.	Dem Frag 2:12	41:53f.	JosAsen 22:2 ftnt b
41:1f.	HelSynPr 12:65	41:54	LAB 8:10

Genesis (cont.)

41:54	HistJos A Recto 25
41:54-57	HistJos A Recto 19
41:55	HistJos A Recto 21
41:56-57	HistJos A Recto 23
42:1	LAB 8:10
42:1-28	Jub 42:4f.
42:3	LAB 8:10
42:3	HistJos A Verso 8
42:6	HistJos A Verso 9
42:6	HistJos A Verso 10
42:6	Dem Frag 2:12 ftnt b
42:7	HistJos A Verso 6
42:7	HistJos A Verso 11
42:7	JosAsen 23:7 ftnt p
42:8	LAB 8:10
42:8	LAB 12:1
42:8	HistJos A Verso 14
42:10	HistJos A Verso 19
42:10	HistJos A Verso 26
42:11	HistJos A Verso 23
42:11	HistJos A Verso 27
42:12	HistJos A Verso 20
42:13	HistJos A Verso 22
42:13	HistJos A Verso 29
42:15	HistJos B Verso 4
42:16	HistJos B Verso 3
42:19	JosAsen 22:7 ftnt i
42:19 (LXX)	JosAsen 26:3 ftnt e
42:19	HistJos B Verso 5
42:20	HistJos B Verso 6-7
42:20	HistJos B Recto 8
42:21-22	HistJos B Verso 10
42:22	HistJos B Verso 12
42:24	HistJos A Verso 16-18
42:24	HistJos B Verso 8
42:25	HistJos B Verso 9
42:28	HistJos A Verso 24-25
42:28	HistJos B Verso 11
42:29	HistJos B Recto 1
42:29-38	Jub 42:9f.
42:30	JosAsen 23:7 ftnt p
42:30	HistJos A Recto 16
42:30	HistJos B Recto 6-8
42:33 (LXX)	JosAsen 26:3 ftnt e
42:36	HistJos B Recto 11-12

43:1–44:2	Jub 42:13f.
43:16	JosAsen 3:4 ftnt g
43:31-34	Dem Frag 2:14
43:32	JosAsen 7:1 ftnt d
43:34	Dem Frag 2:14 ftnt b
44:1	JosAsen 3:4 ftnt g
44:2-34	Jub 43:1f.
44:4	JosAsen 3:4 ftnt g
44:7 (LXX)	JosAsen 23:10 ftnt u
45:1-13	Jub 43:14f.
45:6	Dem Frag 2:12 ftnt c
45:6	Dem Frag 2:17 ftnt a
45:8	JosAsen 20:9 ftnt t
45:15	JosAsen 22:9 ftnt k
45:17-28	Jub 43:21f.
45:22 (LXX)	Dem Frag 2:15 ftnt a
45:22f.	Dem Frag 2:15 ftnt b
45:26	JosAsen 4:7 ftnt j
45:26–46:7	JosAsen 22:2 ftnt b
45:27	JosAsen 19:10 ftnt l
46:1	Jub 44:1f.
46:1–47:12	Art Frag 2 (PrEv 9.23.3)
46:2	JosAsen 14:4 ftnt i
46:2f.	JosAsen 14:6 ftnt j
46:2-4	Jub 44:5f.
46:4	Jub 23:1
46:4	LAB 24:6
46:5-7	Jub 44:7f.
46:8	LAB 8:11
46:8-27	Jub 44:11f.
46:8-27	Dem Frag 2:19 ftnt d
46:8-27	Dem Frag 2:17 ftnt k
46:8-15	Dem Frag 2:14 ftnt d
46:9-15	LAB 8:11
46:10	Jub 34:20
46:10	LAB 8:11 ftnt l
46:10	LAB 8:11 ftnt m
46:11	Dem Frag 2:19 ftnt d
46:11 (LXX)	Dem Frag 2:19 ftnt c
46:15	LAB 8:11 ftnt q
46:15	LAB 8:11 ftnt s
46:16-18	LAB 8:13
46:18	LAB 8:13 ftnt x
46:20	JosAsen 1:2 ftnt e
46:20	JosAsen 1:3 ftnt i
46:20	JosAsen 1:5 ftnt l

46:20-22	LAB 8:14	50:15-26	Jub 46:1f.
46:23-25	LAB 8:12	50:20	JosAsen 28:13 ftnt o
46:24	LAB 8:12 ftnt u	50:22	Dem Frag 2:19
46:25	LAB 8:12 ftnt v	50:22b-26 (LXX)	JosAsen 29:9 ftnt i
46:27	EzekTrag 1	50:26	JosAsen 29:8 ftnt g
46:27	LAB 8:11	50:26	Dem Frag 2:19
46:27	EzekTrag 2 ftnt b	50:26	Art Frag 2 (PrEv
46:27 (LXX)	HelSynPr 12:64		9.23.4)
46:28-34	Jub 44:7f.		
46:29	JosAsen 22:9 ftnt k	*Exodus*	
46:29–47:12	Jub 45:1f.	1:1	LAB 8:11
46:31-34	Dem Frag 2:13	1:1f.	EzekTrag (Intro)
46:34	JosAsen 4:10 ftnt v		ftnt a
47:6-11	PhEPoet Frag 3 ftnt d	1:1-14	Jub 46:11f.
47:7	JosAsen 21:4 ftnt g	1:1–ch. 15	HelSynPr 12:66
47:9	Dem Frag 2:16 ftnt c	1:1f.–Deut	HelSynPr 6:5
47:9	Dem Frag 2:17 ftnt a	1:5 (LXX)	EzekTrag 2 ftnt b
47:13	JosAsen 26:3 ftnt g	1:6	Jub 46:3
47:13-26	Jub 45:8f.	1:6-10	LAB 9:1
47:13-26	JosAsen 4:7 ftnt l	1:7	Jub 46:1
47:22	JosAsen 3:5 ftnt i	1:7	EzekTrag 3
47:25	HistJos A Recto 10	1:8	LAB 9:1 ftnt a
47:26	JosAsen 3:5 ftnt i	1:8	LAB 10:1
47:27	JosAsen 22:2 ftnt b	1:8-14	Art Frag 3 (PrEv
47:28	JosAsen 24:8 ftnt i		9.27.2)
47:28	Dem Frag 2:19	1:9-11	EzekTrag 7
47:28-31	Jub 45:13f.	1:10	3Mac 3:25
47:29	JosAsen 15:13 ftnt e2	1:11	Art Frag 2 (PrEv
48:1f.	PrJos Frag B		9.23.4) ftnt e
48:4	HelSynPr 2:20	1:11 (LXX)	JosAsen 1:2 ftnt e
48:7	PrJos Frag A	1:11 (LXX)	Art Frag 2 (PrEv
48:13	JosAsen 21:6 ftnt j		9.23.3) ftnt d
48:22	Jub 34:7	1:14	EzekTrag 7
49:1–50:41	Jub 45:13f.	1:15-22	EzekTrag 12 ftnt g
49:5-7	JosAsen 22:11 ftnt m	1:22	EzekTrag 12
49:5-7	JosAsen 23:7 ftnt o	1:22	Jub 47:2
49:7	4Mac 2:20	1:22	LAB 9:1
49:9	JosAsen 27:1 ftnt c	1:22	LAB 9:1 ftnt b
49:10	LAB 21:5	1:22	LAB 9:12
49:10	LAB 49:7	1:22	LAB 9:9
49:12	JosAsen 22:7 ftnt h	2:1	Jub 47:1f.
49:24	JosAsen 8:9 ftnt w	2:1-15	EzekTrag 15
49:24 (LXX)	JosAsen 8:9 ftnt w	2:2f.	LAB 9:12
49:33	Jub 23:1	2:2-3	LAB 9:12
49:33	LAB 24:5	2:3	EzekTrag 16 ftnt h
50:1	JosAsen 22:9 ftnt k	2:3	EzekTrag 18
50:10	JosAsen 10:17	2:4f.	LAB 9:15
	ftnt h2	2:5f.	EzekTrag 22
		2:6-8	

6:18	Dem Frag 2:19	10:4f.	EzekTrag 145
6:18	Dem Frag 2:19 ftnt e	10:12-14	Art Frag 3 (PrEv
6:18	Dem Frag 3:2 ftnt c		9.27.32)
6:20	Jub 47:8	10:16	JosAsen 7:4 ftnt i
6:20	LAB 9:3	10:22	EzekTrag 144
6:20	LAB 9:9	11:5	EzekTrag 147
6:20	LAB 9:12	12:1	EzekTrag 189 ftnt b3
6:20	Dem Frag 2:19 ftnt f	12:1f.	Jub 49:1f.
6:20	Dem Frag 2:19 ftnt g	12:1f.–ch. 13	EzekTrag 89 ftnt f2
6:20	Dem Frag 2:19 ftnt i	12:2	EzekTrag 153
6:20 (LXX)	Dem Frag 2:19 ftnt i	12:3	EzekTrag 152
7:1	Art Frag 3 (PrEv	12:3	EzekTrag 175
	9.27.6) ftnt l	12:3	EzekTrag 177 ftnt y2
7:1f.	EzekTrag 89 ftnt f2	12:5	EzekTrag 177
7:1–12:39	Jub 48:5f.	12:5 (LXX)	EzekTrag 177 ftnt y2
7:1–ch. 14	Jub 48:9f.	12:6	EzekTrag 156
7:7	Dem Frag 2:19 ftnt h	12:6	EzekTrag 178
7:8–10:20	Art Frag 3 (PrEv	12:6	Aristob Frag 1:17
	9.27.26)	12:6	Aristob Frag 1:18
7:11	LAB 47:1 ftnt a	12:7	EzekTrag 158
7:12	Art Frag 3 (PrEv	12:8	EzekTrag 160
	9.27.30)	12:11	EzekTrag 180
7:14–12:36	LAB 10:1	12:11	EzekTrag 184 ftnt z2
7:19	EzekTrag 133	12:13	EzekTrag 159
7:20-25	Art Frag 3 (PrEv	12:14	EzekTrag 188
	9.27.28)	12:14-15	EzekTrag 189 ftnt b3
7:22	Art Frag 3 (PrEv	12:15	EzekTrag 189
	9.27.30)	12:17	EzekTrag 154
7:27-8	EzekTrag 135	12:20	EzekTrag 189 ftnt b3
8:2f.	Art Frag 3 (PrEv	12:21	EzekTrag 157
	9.27.32)	12:21	EzekTrag 175
8:10	Art Frag 3 (PrEv	12:21	EzekTrag 176 ftnt x2
	9.27.27	12:21	EzekTrag 177 ftnt y2
8:12	EzekTrag 135	12:21-28	EzekTrag 174
8:17	EzekTrag 138		ftnt w2
8:20	EzekTrag 138	12:22	EzekTrag 185
8:21	Art Frag 3 (PrEv	12:23	EzekTrag 187
	9.27.31)	12:25	EzekTrag 167
9:3 (LXX)	Aristob Frag 2:8	12:29	LAB 32:16
9:3 (LXX)	EzekTrag 2 ftnt b	12:31	Art Frag 3 (PrEv
9:8f.	EzekTrag 136		9.27.34)
9:10	Art Frag 3 (PrEv	12:33	EzekTrag 161
	9.27.31)	12:35-36	EzekTrag 166 ftnt u2
9:11	Jub 48:11	12:35f.	Art Frag 3 (PrEv
9:23	EzekTrag 141		9.27.34)
9:24	Art Frag 3 (PrEv	12:36	Art Frag 3 (PrEv
	9.27.33)		9.27.19) ftnt d2
9:25	EzekTrag 141	12:37f.	EzekTrag 207

Exodus (cont.)

12:37f.	Aristob Frag 2:14
12:40 (LXX)	Dem Frag 2:16
12:40 (LXX)	Dem Frag 2:18
12:40 (LXX)	Dem Frag 2:19 ftnt j
12:40	LAB 9:3
13:2	EzekTrag 172
13:3	EzekTrag 189
13:5	EzekTrag 155
13:5	EzekTrag 171
13:7	EzekTrag 170
13:8	LAB 14:3 ftnt b
13:9 (LXX)	Aristob Frag 2:8
13:15	EzekTrag 172
13:18	LAB 14:1
13:18	Dem Frag 5:1 ftnt d
13:21	LAB 10:7
13:21	FrgsPoetWrks 4 ftnt b
14:1f.	LAB 32:17
14:1f.	Dem Frag 5
14:5-14	Art Frag 3 (PrEv 9.27.35)
14:6f.	EzekTrag 193
14:8	Jub 48:17
14:8	LAB 11:10
14:8	LAB 23:10
14:8-11	LAB 10:2
14:8f.	Jub 48:12
14:9	EzekTrag 204
14:9	EzekTrag 215
14:9	LAB 10:4
14:10	EzekTrag 210
14:11	EzekTrag 212 ftnt k3
14:12	LAB 10:3
14:13	JosAsen 4:8 ftnt r
14:14	JosAsen 28:1 ftnt a
14:15	LAB 10:4
14:15f.	LAB 10:5
14:15-31	Art Frag 3 (PrEv 9.27.36)
14:19	Jub 1:29
14:19f.	EzekTrag 217
14:20	EzekTrag 222 ftnt o3
14:21	EzekTrag 224
14:21	EzekTrag 225 ftnt p3
14:21-31	3Mac 2:7
14:22	LAB 10:6
14:22	LAB 15:5
14:22	EzekTrag 228
14:23	EzekTrag 230
14:23-30	Dem Frag 5:1 ftnt e
14:24	EzekTrag 222 ftnt o3
14:24f.	EzekTrag 233
14:25	JosAsen 28:1 ftnt a
14:25	EzekTrag 239
14:25	LAB 31:1
14:27	EzekTrag 225 ftnt p3
14:28	EzekTrag 242
14:29	HelSynPr 5:9
14:29	LAB 10:6
14:30	EzekTrag 237
15:1f.	JosAsen 21:10 ftnt s
15:1f.	3Mac 2:9
15:1f.	EzekTrag 192 ftnt d3
15:1f.	3Mac 6:4
15:8	LAB 10:5
15:9	LAB 31:1
15:22	Jub 49:23
15:22-27	Dem Frag 4
15:25	LAB 11:15
15:26	EzekTrag 242 ftnt t3
15:27	EzekTrag 243
15:27	EzekTrag 242 ftnt t3
16:1	Jub 50:1f.
16:1f.	HelSynPr 12:75
16:1-36	Art Frag 3 (PrEv 9.27.37)
16:13–17:6	LAB 10:7
16:14	JosAsen 16:8 ftnt f
16:31	JosAsen 16:8 ftnt f
17:1f.	HelSynPr 12:74
17:6	Aristob Frag 2:9
17:8-13	LAB 27:10 ftnt d
17:8-13	Dem Frag 5:1 ftnt c
17:14	LAB 58:1
17:16 (LXX)	JosAsen 8:9 ftnt d2
18:1-12	Dem Frag 3:3 ftnt b
18:1f.	Dem Frag 3:1 ftnt c
18:21	JosAsen 4:7 ftnt p
18:21f.	Ps-Phoc 86
19:1	Jub 6:11
19:1	LAB 11:1
19:1f.	LAB 32:7
19:2	Aristob Frag 2:14

19:4	FrgsPoetWrks 4	20:17	Ps-Phoc 6f.
	ftnt e	20:18	LAB 11:14
19:6	Jub 16:18	20:18	HelSynPr 5:13
19:11	Aristob Frag 2:12	20:18	Aristob Frag 2:13
19:14f.	LAB 11:3	20:18	FrgsPoetWrks 4
19:15	LAB 11:2		ftnt d
19:16	FrgsPoetWrks 4 ftnt f	20:19f.	LAB 11:14
19:16f.	LAB 11:4	20:21	LAB 11:15
19:16-19	Aristob Frag 2:13	20:23	JosAsen 2:3 ftnt f
19:17	Aristob Frag 2:14	20:25	Ps-Hec Frag 4
19:18	FrgsPoetWrks 4		(1.198) ftnt m
	ftnt b	20:26	Jub 3:28
19:18	FrgsPoetWrks 4 ftnt i	21:22f. (LXX)	Ps-Phoc 185 ftnt i
20:1f.	LAB 11:6	21:24	Jub 4:31
20:1f.	HelSynPr 5:13	22:4f.	Ps-Phoc 35
20:1f.	HelSynPr 12:69	22:4f.	Ps-Phoc 38
20:2-17	LAB 44:6	22:6-12	Ps-Phoc 12f.
20:4-6	LAB 11:6	22:16	Ps-Phoc 198
20:5	Jub 20:8	22:19	Ps-Phoc 188
20:5f.	JosAsen 11:7 ftnt v	22:21	OdesSol 20:5
20:7	LAB 11:7	22:24	4Mac 2:9
20:7	Ps-Phoc 16-17	22:24	Ps-Phoc 83 ftnt f
20:8	HelSynPr 5:14	22:25f.	Ah 171
20:8	Jub 2:26	22:26f.	OdesSol 20:6
20:8	LAB 11:8 ftnt g	22:27 (LXX)	JosAsen 10:12 ftnt v
20:8-11	Aristob Frag 5:9	22:31	Ps-Phoc 148 ftnt h
20:8-11	LAB 11:8	23:1-3	Ps-Phoc 9 ftnt a
20:8-11	HelSynPr 5:1	23:4	Ps-Phoc 141 ftnt d
20:9	Ps-Phoc 153	23:4f.	4Mac 2:14
20:9f.	Jub 50:7	23:5	Ps-Phoc 140 ftnt c
20:11	Jub 2:16	23:6	Ps-Phoc 10 ftnt b
20:11	LAB 11:8 ftnt h	23:9	Ps-Phoc 40 ftnt g
20:11 (LXX)	Aristob Frag 5:12	23:12	Aristob Frag 5:9
20:12	LAB 11:9	23:16	Jub 6:21
20:12	Ah 138	23:33	Jub 1:9
20:12	Ps-Phoc 6f.	24:10	Jub 1:28
20:12	SyrMen 10	24:12	Jub Title
20:13	Ps-Phoc 4	24:17	Aristob Frag 2:13
20:13	SyrMen 15	24:18	LAB 11:15
20:13	SyrMen 240	25:1–ch. 31	LAB 11:15
20:14	LAB 11:10	25:8	Jub 1:17
20:14	Ps-Phoc 3	25:8	LAB 11:15
20:15	LAB 11:11	25:9	LAB 11:15
20:16	LAB 11:12	25:9	LivPro 3:15
20:16	Ps-Phoc 12f.	25:31-40	Ps-Hec Frag 4
20:16	SyrMen 144		(1.198) ftnt n
20:17	LAB 11:13	25:31-40	Eup 34:5 ftnt p
20:17	4Mac 2:5	26:1	JosAsen 2:8 ftnt m

Exodus (cont.)

26:31	JosAsen 2:8 ftnt m
26:32	Eup 34:3 ftnt k
26:36	JosAsen 2:8 ftnt m
27:1-2	Eup 34:8 ftnt s
27:21	Jub 2:33
27:21	Eup 34:5 ftnt p
28:4	LetAris 96
28:5f.	JosAsen 2:8 ftnt m
28:8	JosAsen 2:8 ftnt m
28:15	JosAsen 2:8 ftnt m
28:17-20	LAB 26:10
28:27-31	LetAris 96
28:30	LAB 22:8
28:30	LivPro 22:2 ftnt c
28:42	Jub 3:28
29:40	Jub 6:3
29:45	Jub 1:17
30:1-5	Ps-Hec Frag 4
	(1.198) ftnt n
30:10	3Mac 1:12
30:12	4Mac 3:21
30:14	Jub 49:17
30:17-21	Eup 34:7 ftnt r
30:18	LAB 11:15 ftnt o
30:34	Jub 3:27
30:34	Jub 16:24
31:13	Jub 2:17
31:13	Jub 2:19
31:13	Jub 2:21
31:13	Jub 2.26
31:14f.	Jub 2:25
31:17	Jub 2:19
31:17	Jub 2:21
31:18	Jub 1:1
32:1f.	LAB 12:2
32:2-4	LAB 12:3
32:7	LAB 12:4 ftnt c
32:7f.	LAB 12:4
32:15	Jub 1:1
32:15	LAB 12:5
32:19	LAB 12:5
32:19	LAB 19:7
32:20	LAB 12:7
32:30	JosAsen 28:7 ftnt f
32:32f.	JosAsen 15:4 ftnt g
33:1	Jub 1:7
33:20	AscenIs 3:9
34:1	LAB 12:10
34:6	JosAsen 11:10
	ftnt d2
34:22	Jub 6:17
34:27	Jub 1:26
34:27	Jub 1:5
34:27f.	LAB 12:10 ftnt k
34:28	JosAsen 10:1 ftnt c
34:29-35	LAB 12:1
35:1–ch. 40	LAB 13:1
35:2	Jub 2:25
35:2	JosAsen 21:8 ftnt p
35:3	Jub 2:29
35:15f.	LAB 13:1 ftnt b
37:17-24	Ps-Hec Frag 4
	(1.198) ftnt n
37:25-28	Ps-Hec Frag 4
	(1.198) ftnt n
38:24-31	Eup 34:14 ftnt y
40:33f.	LAB 13:2

Leviticus

1:1	LAB 13:2
1:10	LAB 13:2
1:14	LAB 13:2
2:2-5	Jub 6:3
3:1	EzekTrag 177 ftnt y2
3:7-10	Jub 21:7
3:11	Jub 21:9
5:20-26	Ps-Phoc 12f.
7:26	Jub 21:5
7:27	Jub 7:28
7:36	Jub 2:33
11:1-23	4Mac 5:26
11:22	LivPro 2:7 ftnt k
12:2-5	Jub 3:8
14:2-6	LAB 13:3
16:29	Jub 34:18
16:34	Jub 34:18
16:34	3Mac 1:12
17:7	Jub 7:21
17:10	Jub 6:11
17:10	Jub 7:32
17:11	Jub 6:14
17:11	Jub 7:32
17:12	Jub 6:11
17:13	Jub 7:30
17:13f.	Jub 21:18

17:14	Jub 7:32	25:2-7	Jub 7:37
18:2	Jub 31:16	25:8	Jub 50:2
18:4	Jub 31:16	25:36	Ps-Phoc 83 ftnt f
18:5	PssSol 14:3	25:36-53	4Mac 2:9
18:8	Ps-Phoc 179	26:2-5	LAB 13:10
18:8	Ps-Phoc 181 ftnt f	26:12	Jub 1:17
18:15	Jub 41:26	26:17f.	HelSynPr 10:10
18:18	Jub 28:6	26:34	Jub 50:3
18:19	Ps-Phoc 189 ftnt m	26:40	Jub 1:22
18:22	Ps-Phoc 4	26:44	3Mac 6:15
18:23	Ps-Phoc 188	27:32	Jub 32:15
18:26-28	Jub 6:2	27:32	LAB 5:4 ftnt b
19:3	Ps-Phoc 6f.		
19:3	Ps-Phoc 19-21	*Numbers*	
19:8	PssSol 1:8	1:1-3	LAB 14:1
19:12	Ps-Phoc 16-17	1:45-47	Aristob Frag 2:14
19:15	Ps-Phoc 9 ftnt a	1:46	LAB 14:3 ftnt b
19:23f.	Jub 7:36	1:46-49	LAB 14:3
19:26	Jub 7:31	2:33	LAB 14:3
19:29	Ps-Phoc 177 ftnt c	3:17 (LXX)	Dem Frag 2:19 ftnt c
19:32	Ps-Phoc 220	3:19	Dem Frag 2:19 ftnt e
19:32	SyrMen 13	3:19	Dem Frag 3:2 ftnt c
19:33f.	Ps-Phoc 39	3:39	LAB 14:3 ftnt d
19:34	Ps-Phoc 40 ftnt g	5:11-31	LAB 12:7 ftnt f
19:35f.	Ps-Phoc 12f.	5:19	PssSol 8:10 ftnt f
20:10	Jub 20:4	9:1	LAB 14:5
20:11	Jub 33:10	9:13	Jub 49:9
20:11	Ps-Phoc 179	10:29	Dem Frag 3:1 ftnt f
20:12	Jub 41:26	11:21	Aristob Frag 2:14
20:13	Ps-Phoc 4	11:26	LAB 20:5
20:14	Jub 41:26	11:31	HelSynPr 12:74
20:15f.	Ps-Phoc 188	11:35–12:2	Dem Frag 3:3
21:6 (LXX)	PssSol 2:3 ftnt e	12:1	Dem Frag 3:3 ftnt d
21:9	Jub 20:4	12:1	EzekTrag 60 ftnt x
23:1f.	HelSynPr 5:16	12:8	LAB 11:14
23:4-8	LAB 13:4	13:1-3	LAB 15:1
23:14	Jub 2:33	13:20-29	LAB 15:1
23:15-20	Jub 15:2	13:22	Jub 13:12
23:15-21	LAB 13:5	13:22	LivPro 6:3 ftnt f
23:24	Jub 6:23	13:32f.	LAB 15:1
23:24-32	LAB 13:6	13:30	LAB 15:2
23:34-44	Jub 32:4	14:3	LAB 10:2
23:40	LAB 13:7	14:3	LAB 15:4
23:40-42	Jub 16:29	14:10	LAB 15:5
24:16	JosAsen 11:15 ftnt o2	14:13-19	LAB 15:7
24:22	Ps-Phoc 39	14:30-34	Eup 30:1 ftnt d
25:1f.	HelSynPr 5:17	14:32	LAB 15:6
		14:35	LAB 20:3

Numbers (cont.)

15:32-36	Jub 2:25
15:37-41	LAB 16:1 ftnt c
15:37–16:3	LAB 16:1
16:1	Dem Frag 3:2 ftnt c
16:1-3	LAB 16:1 ftnt c
16:1f.	LAB 53:9
16:2	LAB 16:1 ftnt b
16:14	JosAsen 10:1 ftnt a
16:15	LAB 57:2
16:22	Jub 10:3
16:23-30	4Mac 2:17
16:26	Ps-Phoc 134
16:26f.	LAB 16:7
16:30	LAB 16:3
16:32	LAB 16:6
16:32	LAB 57:2
16:48 (LXX)	HelSynPr 6:6
17:1-15	4Mac 7:11
17:2	LAB 17:1
17:4f.	LAB 17:1
17:7f.	LAB 17:2
20:1f.	HelSynPr 12:74
21:1	Art Frag 3 (PrEv 9.27.7) ftnt m
21:1f.	LAB 18:1
21:16-20	LAB 10:7
21:29	LAB 18:12 ftnt u
22:2f.	LAB 18:1
22:5	LAB 18:1
22:6	LAB 18:2
22:8	LAB 18:3
22:9	LAB 18:4
22:12	LAB 18:6
22:13 (LXX)	LAB 18:7 ftnt i
22:13-15	LAB 18:7
22:17	LAB 18:2
22:18	LAB 18:3
22:18	Ah 131 ftnt i
22:19-21	LAB 18:8
22:19	LAB 23:2
22:27	LAB 18:9
22:31	LAB 18:9 ftnt m
22:31f.	LAB 18:9
22:35	LAB 18:9
22:41	LAB 18:10
23:2	LAB 18:10
23:2	LAB 18:10 ftnt n
23:6	LAB 18:10 ftnt o
23:6f.	LAB 18:10
23:10	LAB 28:10
24:2	LAB 18:11
24:10f.	LAB 18:12
24:13	Ah 131 ftnt i
24:17	LAB 28:6
24:17	Jub 22:12
24:25	LAB 18:14
25:1	LAB 18:14
25:1f.	LAB 18:13
25:1f.	LAB 30:1
25:6-18	LAB 47:1
25:7-13	4Mac 18:12
26:11	LAB 16:5
26:57 (LXX)	Dem Frag 2:19 ftnt c
26:58f.	Dem Frag 2:19 ftnt f
26:59	Jub 47:8
26:59	Dem Frag 2:19 ftnt e
27:1-11	JosAsen 2:1 ftnt b
27:12	LAB 19:8
27:16	Jub 10:3
27:21	LivPro 22:2 ftnt c
28:3-8	Jub 6:14
28:26	Jub 6:21
29:2-5	Jub 7:3
29:12-40	Jub 16:20f.
29:12-40	Jub 32:4
31:16	LAB 18:13
31:27	LAB 19:1
32:12	LAB 15:3
35:27f.	JosAsen 15:7 ftnt l
35:33	Jub 7:33
35:33	Jub 21:19
35:33f.	Jub 6:2
36:1f.	LAB 29:1

Deuteronomy

1:13	Ps-Phoc 86
1:17	Ps-Phoc 9 ftnt b
1:22f.	LAB 15:1 ftnt a
1:31	HelSynPr 5:12
2:23	Jub 24:30
3:28	LAB 20:2
4:11	Aristob Frag 2:13
4:12	Aristob Frag 4:3
4:20	Jub 16:18
4:20	Jub 22:9

4:20	HelSynPr 5:9	10:17	PssSol 2:18
4:26	LAB 19:4	11:9	LAB 21:9
4:26	LAB 24:1	12:23	Jub 6:12
4:28	Jub 1:14	12:23	Jub 21:18
4:29f.	Jub 1:15	13:9f.	PssSol 4:3
4:33	Aristob Frag 4:3	14:1	Jub 1:24
4:39	HelSynPr 4:26	14:22f.	Jub 32:10
5:6-21	LAB 44:6	15:1	Jub 7:37
5:9f.	JosAsen 11:7 ftnt v	15:9	Jub 7:37
5:11	Ps-Phoc 16-17	15:9	4Mac 2:9
5:12	LAB 11:8 ftnt g	15:1-18	4:Mac 2:8 ftnt a
5:12-15	Aristob Frag 5:9	15:11	Ps-Phoc 28f.
5:16	Ah 138	15:14	Ps-Phoc 28f.
5:16	Ps-Phoc 6f.	16:2	EzekTrag 177 ftnt y2
5:16	SyrMen 10	16:5-7	Jub 49:20
5:17	Ps-Phoc 4	16:7	EzekTrag 177 ftnt y2
5:17	SyrMen 15	16:18-20	Ps-Phoc 9 ftnt a
5:17	SyrMen 240	17:15	LAB 56:1
5:18	Ps-Phoc 3	18:18	Aristob Frag 2:4
5:20	Ps-Phoc 12f.	20:19	4Mac 2:14
5:20	SyrMen 144	21:18-21	SyrMen 44
5:21	Ps-Phoc 6f.	21:18-21	Ps-Phoc 209 ftnt a
5:22	LAB 11:14	22:6	LAB 53:10
5:23	Aristob Frag 2:13	22:6f.	Ps-Phoc 85 ftnt g
5:23-26	Aristob Frag 4:3	22:23	Jub 20:4
5:27	LAB 19:4	22:30	Jub 33:7
5:31f.	Jub 23:16	22:30	Jub 33:12
5:32	LAB 38:2	23:20	4Mac 2:9
6:4	Ps-Orph 10	23:20	Ps-Phoc 83 ftnt f
6:4	Aristob Frag 4:5	23:25	Ps-Phoc 35
6:4	LAB 23:2	23:25	Ps-Phoc 38
6:4	FrgsPoetWrks 5	24:10-13	Ah 172
	ftnt b	24:14	Ps-Phoc 19-21
7:3f.	JosAsen 7:5 ftnt k	25:4	Ah 192 ftnt a
7:6	HelSynPr 5:8	25:19	LAB 58:1
7:12f.	PssSol 1:3 ftnt c	25:14f.	Ps-Phoc 12f.
7:13	Jub 20:9	26:14	Jub 22:17
8:13f.	Ah 137	27:5f.	Ps-Hec Frag 4
9:11	Jub 1:1		(1.198) ftnt m
9:15	Aristob Frag 2:13	27:15	Jub 20:8
9:26	Jub 1:19	27:18	Ps-Phoc 24-25
9:26	Jub 1:21	27:21	Ps-Phoc 188
9:29	Jub 1:21	27:24	Jub 4:5
10:10	LAE Vita 6:3	28:8	Jub 20:9
10:16	Jub 1:23	28:14	LAB 25:3
10:16	OdesSol 11:1 ftnt a	28:26	PssSol 4:19 ftnt n
10:17	Jub 5:16	28:36	Jub 1:14
10:17	Jub 21:4	28:62	LAB 14:2

Deuteronomy (cont.)

28:64	Jub 1:14	1:6	LAB 20:5
29:5	Eup 30:1 ftnt c	1:7	LAB 25:3
29:17	LAB 25:3	1:7f.	LAB 38:2
29:28	Jub 2:27	1:8	LAB 22:6
30:1	Jub 1:6	1:9	LAB 20:5
30:6	Jub 1:23	2:1	LAB 20:6
30:6	OdesSol 11:1 ftnt a	3:13-17	LAE Vita 8:3
30:19	JosAsen 24:7 ftnt g	5:1f.	HelSynPr 6:6
30:20	Jub 1:7	5:4	FrgsPoetWrks 4 ftnt i
31:1–ch. 34	LAB 19:2 ftnt a	5:12	LAB 20:8
31:6	Jub 1:18	5:14	JosAsen 14:8 ftnt k
31:16	LAB 19:6	5:14	JosAsen 14:8 ftnt l
31:16	LAB 21:1	5:14	PrJos Frag A
31:16-18	LAB 19:1	6:24	LAB 20:7
31:20	Jub 1:7	7:1	LAB 21:3
31:23	LAB 20:1	7:7	LAB 21:3
31:27	Jub 1:7	8:30-35	LAB 21:7
31:27	Jub 1:22	8:31	LAB 21:8
31:28	JosAsen 19:6 ftnt e	8:31	LAB 21:9
32:1	LAB 19:4	8:33	LAB 21:7 ftnt d
32:2	FrgsPoetWrks 4	9:8	JosAsen 24:15 ftnt q
	ftnt b	9:11	JosAsen 24:15 ftnt q
32:6	3Mac 2:21	10:9	JosAsen 27:6 ftnt i
32:8f.	Jub 15:31	10:11	LAB 30:5 ftnt f
32:10	JosAsen 25:5 ftnt i	10:11-13	LAB 30:5
32:39	4Mac 18:19	10:12	LAB 32:10
32:49	LAB 19:8	10:12f.	PssSol 18:12
32:52	LAB 19:7	11:21f.	LivPro 6:3 ftnt f
33:1f.	LAB 19:5	11:22	LivPro 6:3
33:2	Jub 1:27	12:7-24	LAB 20:9
33:3 (LXX)	4Mac 17:19	12:24	LAB 20:9 ftnt c
33:3	HelSynPr 4:28	13:1	LAB 21:1
33:3	HelSynPr 16:10	13:1–ch. 23	LAB 20:9
33:17	JosAsen 16:17 ftnt a2	14:6	LAB 20:10
34:1	LAB 19:10	14:6-8	LAB 20:6
34:4	LAB 19:7	14:7	Eup 30:1 ftnt d
34:4	LAB 19:10	14:8	LAB 15:1
34:5f.	LAB 19:16	14:8f.	LAB 20:10
34:6	LAB 19:12	14:13	LAB 20:10
34:7	Art Frag 3 (PrEv	15:46f.	LAB 29:2
	9.27.37) ftnt y2	16:1f.	Dem Frag 2:10 ftnt a
		17:11	Eup 39:5 ftnt d
34:10	Aristob Frag 2:4	17:11	LivPro 5:1 ftnt a
		17:16	Eup 39:5 ftnt d
Joshua		18:13 (LXX)	Dem Frag 2:10 ftnt a
1:1-3	LAB 20:2	18:22	LivPro 19:1 ftnt b
1:1f.	JosAsen 1:1 ftnt b	19:1	LAB 25:2
1:1–ch. 13	HelSynPr 12:77	19:51	LAB 23:1

21:19	LivPro 21:1 ftnt d	3:15	LAB 29:1 ftnt a
22:10	LAB 22:1 ftnt q	4:1f.	HelSynPr 6:7
22:10-12	LAB 22:1	4:1f.	HelSynPr 6:12
22:13	LAB 22:1 ftnt d	4:2f.	LAB 30:3
22:15	LAB 22:1 ftnt d	4:3	LAB 30:3 ftnt c
22:15-20	LAB 22:2	4:5	LAB 30:4 ftnt d
22:21	LAB 22:3	4:6	LAB 31:1
22:23	LAB 22:1 ftnt b	4:9	LAB 31:2
22:24f.	LAB 22:3	4:9	LAB 31:7
22:26	LAB 22:1 ftnt b	4:11	Dem Frag 3:1 ftnt b
22:28	LAB 22:1 ftnt b	4:11	Dem Frag 3:1 ftnt f
22:29	LAB 22:1 ftnt b	4:15	LAB 31:3
23:1	LAB 21:1	4:17	LAB 31:3 ftnt b
23:2	LAB 23:1	4:17	LAB 31:3 ftnt c
23:13	Jub 1:10	4:17f.	LAB 31:3
23:14	LAB 33:2	4:19	LAB 31:4
24:1 (LXX)	LAB 23:1 ftnt b	4:19	LAB 31:5
24:1f.	LAB 23:2	4:21	LAB 31:7
24:2	LAB 23:4	4:21	LAB 31:7
24:2	LAB 23:4	4:21-22	PssSol 4:15 ftnt k
24:3	LAB 23:5	4:22	LAB 31:9
24:3	LAB 23:8	5:1	LAB 32:1
24:4f.	LAB 23:9	5:1f.	HelSynPr 6:7
24:13	LAB 23:11	5:4f.	FrgsPoetWrks 4 ftnt f
24:15	LAB 24:1	5:7	LAB 33:6
24:17f.	LAB 23:14	5:15-16	LAB 10:3 ftnt b
24:24	LAB 23:9 ftnt f	5:20	LAB 31:1
24:24	LAB 23:14	5:20	LAB 31:2
24:28	LAB 24:3	5:20	LAB 32:17
24:28	LAB 24:6	5:24	LAB 32:12
24:29	Eup 30:1 ftnt d	5:25	LAB 31:4
24:30	LAB 24:6	5:26	LAB 31:7
		5:26	LAB 31:7
Judges		5:28	LAB 31:3
1:1	LAB 25:1	5:28	LAB 31:8 ftnt d
1:1f.	JosAsen 1:1 ftnt b	5:28-30	LAB 31:7
1:16	Dem Frag 3:1 ftnt b	5:30	LAB 31:1
1:16	Dem Frag 3:1 ftnt f	5:31	LAB 32:18
1:20	LAB 20:10 ftnt d	5:31	LAB 33:6
2:1-3	LAB 30:2	6:1	LAB 34:5
2:3	LAB 30:2	6:1f.	HelSynPr 6:7
2:10	Jub 23:2	6:1-6	LAB 34:1
2:17	LAB 30:1	6:7-10	LAB 34:4
2:17	LAB 30:2	6:11f.	LAB 35:1
3:8-11	LAB 27:16	6:12	LAB 35:1 ftnt a
3:9	LivPro 10:10	6:13	LAB 35:2
3:9	LAB 25:2 ftnt c	6:13	LAB 35:3
3:11	LAB 25:2 ftnt c	6:14	LAB 35:3

Judges (cont.)

6:14	LAB 35:4
6:15	LAB 35:1
6:15	LAB 35:5
6:16	LAB 35:5
6:17	LAB 35:6
6:17	LAB 35:6
6:20	LAB 35:6
6:20f.	LAB 35:7
6:21	LAB 42:9
6:21	JosAsen 17:3 ftnt c
6:21	JosAsen 17:8 ftnt h
6:21f.	JosAsen 17:8 ftnt j
6:25-32	JosAsen 10:12 ftnt v
6:25-32	LAB 36:4
6:34	LAB 36:2
7:8	LAB 27:5
7:9-18	LAB 27:6
7:14	LAB 36:1
7:15	LAB 36:2
7:16 (LXX)	JosAsen 24:20 ftnt z
7:19	LAB 36:1
7:19f.	LAB 36:2
8:1f.	HelSynPr 6:7
8:10	LAB 36:2
8:24-27	LAB 36:3
8:26	LAB 36:3 ftnt e
8:32	LAB 36:4
9:1	LAB 37:1
9:5	LAB 37:1
9:8-15	LAB 37:2 ftnt d
9:8-15	Ah 166 ftnt m
9:8f.	LAB 37:2 ftnt c
9:10f.	LAB 37:2
9:12f.	LAB 37:2
9:14	LAB 37:3
9:15	LAB 37:3
9:15	LAB 37:4
9:18	LAB 37:1
9:22	LAB 37:4
9:28-41	LAB 29:1
9:53	LAB 37:5
10:3-6	LAB 38:1
10:9	LAB 39:1
10:13	LAB 39:6
10:17f.	LAB 39:1
11:1-3	LAB 39:2
11:1f.	HelSynPr 6:7
11:2	LAB 39:2 ftnt a
11:3	LAB 39:3 ftnt b
11:5f.	LAB 39:3
11:7	LAB 39:4
11:11	LAB 39:6
11:12	LAB 39:8
11:14	LAB 39:9
11:24	LAB 39:9
11:28	LAB 39:10
11:29	LAB 39:8
11:30f.	LAB 39:10
11:31	LAB 39:11
11:32-35	LAB 40:1
11:33	LAB 40:1 ftnt a
11:36	LAB 40:2
11:36-38	LAB 40:3
11:38	LAB 40:4
11:39f.	LAB 40:8
12:7	LAB 40:9
12:11f.	LAB 41:2
12:13-15	LAB 41:1
12:15	LAB 41:1 ftnt b
13:1	LAB 41:3
13:1f.	HelSynPr 6:7
13:2	LAB 42:1
13:3	LAB 42:3
13:3	LAB 42:3
13:4	LAB 42:3
13:6	LAB 42:4
13:6	JosAsen 15:12 ftnt c2
13:8	LAB 42:5
13:8f.	LivPro 16:3 ftnt c
13:9f.	LAB 42:6
13:10-12	LAB 42:7
13:14	LAB 42:3
13:15f.	LAB 42:8
13:15f.	JosAsen 15:14 ftnt f2
13:16f.	JosAsen 15:12 ftnt c2
13:16-18	LAB 42:10
13:17	JosAsen 15:12 ftnt d2
13:19	LAB 42:9
13:20	LAB 42:9
13:20-22	JosAsen 17:8 ftnt j
13:22	LAB 42:10
13:23	LAB 42:9
13:24	LAB 42:3
13:24	LAB 43:1
14:1f.	LAB 43:1

14:5f.	LAB 43:4	20:24f.	LAB 46:3
14:12	JosAsen 21:8 ftnt n	20:25	LAB 46:3 ftnt c
14:17	JosAsen 21:8 ftnt n	20:26	LAB 46:3
15:4f.	LAB 43:4	20:26-28	LAB 46:4
15:6	LAB 43:1	20:27f.	LAB 46:1
15:14	LAB 43:4	20:28	LAB 46:3
15:15f.	LAB 43:4	20:31-37	LAB 47:9
15:18-19	HelSynPr 6:7	20:37	LAB 47:10
16:1	LAB 43:5	20:41-43	LAB 47:10
16:1-3	LAB 43:2	20:42	LAB 47:9
16:3	LAB 43:3	20:46-48	LAB 47:10
16:4	LAB 43:5	21:17-19	LAB 48:3
16:16	LAB 43:6	21:23	LAB 48:3
16:16f.	LAB 43:6	21:25	LAB 48:4
16:19	LAB 43:6		
16:21	LAB 43:6	*Ruth*	
16:25	LAB 43:7	1:1f.	JosAsen 1:1 ftnt b
16:25	PssSol 3:2	1:14	LAB 61:6
16:27	LAB 43:8 ftnt e	1:16f.	JosAsen 20:4 ftnt g
16:28	LAB 43:5	3:7	PssSol 3:2
16:28	LAB 43:7		
16:29	LAB 43:3 ftnt b	*1 Samuel*	
16:29-31	LAB 43:8	1:1	LAB 49:4 ftnt d
16:30	LAB 43:7	1:1f.	HelSynPr 6:12
17:1-4	LAB 44:1	1:1–ch. 4	Eup 30:8 ftnt u
17:1f.	LivPro 6:1 ftnt b	1:2	LAB 50:1
17:5	LAB 44:5	1:3	LAB 50:2
17:6	LAB 44:1	1:6	LAB 50:1
18:6	JosAsen 20:10 ftnt u	1:7	LAB 50:2
18:12 (LXX)	LivPro 1:9 ftnt n	1:8	LAB 49:7
19:1	LAB 45:1	1:8f.	LAB 50:3
19:2	LAB 45:3	1:10	LAB 50:2
19:13	LAB 45:1	1:11	JosAsen 11:12 ftnt j2
19:14	LAB 45:1	1:13	LAB 50:5
19:15	LAB 45:1	1:14	LAB 50:6 ftnt g
19:16-20	LAB 45:2	1:14	LAB 50:6 ftnt h
19:17	LAB 35:1	1:14f.	LAB 50:6
19:22-25	LAB 45:3	1:15	LAB 50:7
19:27-29	LAB 45:4	1:17	Jub 18:16
20:1	LAB 45:5	1:17	LAB 50:7
20:5	LAB 45:4	1:18	JosAsen 13:9 ftnt h
20:6	LAB 45:5	1:18	LAB 50:8
20:11	LAB 46:1	1:19	LAB 50:8 ftnt j
20:12f.	LAB 46:2	1:20	LAB 51:1
20:13	LAB 46:1	1:23f.	LAB 51:1
20:18	LAB 43:5 ftnt f	1:24	LAB 51:1 ftnt c
20:21	LAB 46:2	1:24f.	LivPro 18:1
20:23	LAB 46:3	1:25f.	LAB 51:2

1 Samuel (cont.)

1:26	LAB 51:2 ftnt d
2:1	LAB 51:3
2:3	LAB 51:4
2:3	Ps-Phoc 122
2:3	HelSynPr 4:28
2:5	LAB 50:5
2:5	LAB 51:4
2:6	LAB 51:4
2:7	LAB 50:2
2:8	PssSol 2:19 ftnt r
2:9	LAB 51:5
2:10	LAB 50:2
2:10	LAB 51:3
2:10f.	LAB 51:6
2:11	LAB 51:7
2:11	LAB 53:1
2:11-16	LAB 52:1
2:16	JosAsen 24:19 ftnt x
2:23f.	LAB 52:2
2:25	LAB 52:3
2:25	LAB 52:4
2:34	LAB 52:1
3:1	LAB 53:1
3:1-14	JosAsen 4:3 ftnt e
3:3	LAB 53:2
3:4f.	LAB 53:3
3:5	LAB 53:4
3:6	LAB 53:5
3:7	LAB 53:1
3:7	LAB 53:2
3:8	LAB 53:7
3:8f.	LAB 53:5
3:9f.	JosAsen 24:4 ftnt d
3:9	LAB 53:6
3:11	LAB 53:6
3:15	LAB 53:12
3:15	LAB 53:13
3:17	LAB 53:12
3:18	LAB 53:13
4:1-3	LAB 54:1
4:5	LAB 54:2
4:10f.	LAB 54:3
4:12	LAB 54:4
4:14-17	LAB 54:4
4:18	LAB 54:5
4:19-21	LAB 54:6
5:2-6	LAB 55:3
5:3f.	LAB 55:4
5:7	LAB 55:4
5:10f.	LAB 55:4
6:2	LAB 55:5
6:2	LAB 55:7
6:4	LAB 55:2
6:7-10	LAB 55:6
6:9	LAB 55:7
6:9	LAB 55:7
6:10-12	LAB 55:8
6:12	LAB 55:9 ftnt e
6:17	LAB 55:9
6:19	LAB 55:9
6:21	LAB 55:9
7:1f.	HelSynPr 6:7
7:17	LAB 55:1
8:4f.	LAB 56:1
8:5	LAB 57:4
8:6	LAB 56:2
8:6	LAB 56:7
8:9	LAB 56:3
9:1-4	LAB 56:4
9:9	LAB 56:4
9:12f.	LAB 56:4
9:16	LAB 56:3
9:18	LAB 56:4
9:19	LAB 56:4
9:19	LAB 56:4
9:19	LAB 59:2
9:21	LAB 56:6
9:24-26	LAB 56:5
10:1	LAB 56:5
10:6	LAB 20:2
10:8	LAB 56:7 ftnt c
10:9	LAB 56:7
12:1-3	LAB 57:1
12:3	LAB 57:3
12:5	LAB 57:3
13:1	Eup 30:2 ftnt f
13:9	LAB 57:5
13:17 (LXX)	JosAsen 24:20 ftnt z
14:45	LAB 63:3
15:3	LAB 30:4
15:3	LAB 58:1
15:5	JosAsen 24:19 ftnt s
15:7-9	LAB 58:2
15:12f.	LAB 58:3-4
15:16	LAB 58:2

15:20	LAB 58:2	20:14	JosAsen 23:3 ftnt i
15:20	LAB 58:2	20:23	LAB 62:10
15:27	LAB 64:6	20:41f.	LAB 62:11
15:33f.	LAB 58:4	22:4 (LXX)	PhEPoet Frags 1-2
16:1	LAB 59:1		ftnt h
16:1-11	Ps 151A (Heb):5	22:9-13	LAB 63:2
16:3	LAB 59:1	22:16-21	LAB 63:2
16:4-7	LAB 59:2	22:18	LAB 63:3
16:10	Ps 151A (Heb):6	22:18f.	LAB 63:1
16:10	Ps 151A (Syr):5	22:19	LAB 30:4
16:11	Ps 151A (Heb):1	24:16	JosAsen 28:7 ftnt g
16:11	Ps 151A (Syr):1	25:1	LAB 64:1
16:11-13	LAB 59:3	25:32	JosAsen 3:3 ftnt f
16:12f.	Ps 151A (Heb):7	25:41	JosAsen 7:1 ftnt b
16:14	LAB 60:1	28:3	LAB 64:1
16:19	LAB 60:1	28:3	LAB 64:1
16:23	LAB 60:1	28:4	LAB 64:3
16:23	LAB 60:3	28:5-7	LAB 64:3
17:1f. (esp. 48-51)	JosAsen 27:1 ftnt a	28:8-11	LAB 64:4
17:4	LAB 61:2	28:12f.	LAB 64:5
17:8-25	Ps 151B (Heb):1	28:13f.	LAB 64:6
17:9	LAB 61:2	28:14	LAB 64:7
17:11	LAB 61:2	28:15	LAB 64:7
17:14	Ps 151A (Heb):1	28:19	LAB 64:8
17:15	LAB 61:1	28:22f.	JosAsen 15:14 ftnt f2
17:16	LAB 61:3	28:25	LAB 64:9
17:22	LAB 61:3	30:12	JosAsen 10:1 ftnt c
17:23	JosAsen 19:1 ftnt a	31:1	LAB 65:1
17:28	LAB 61:3	31:1f.	LAB 63:3
17:31	LAB 61:4	31:3	LAB 65:1
17:32	LAB 61:4	31:4	LAB 65:2
17:34	LAB 59:5 ftnt f	31:4	LAB 65:3
17:34-36	Ps 152:2	31:6	LAB 62:2
17:34-36	Ps 153:2	31:13	JosAsen 10:17 ftnt h2
17:34-37	LAB 59:5		
17:36	LAB 61:4	*2 Samuel*	
17:36-38	Ps 151A (Syr):1	1:1f.	JosAsen 1:1 ftnt b
17:40	LAB 61:4	1:2	JosAsen 10:14 ftnt b2
17:49-51	LAB 61:7	1:7	LAB 65:3
17:50f.	JosAsen 29:2 ftnt a	1:8	LAB 65:4
17:51	Ps 151B (Syr):2	1:9	LAB 65:3
17:55-58	LAB 61:9	1:10	LAB 65:4
18:3	LAB 62:1	1:10	LAB 65:4
18:3	LAB 62:3	1:13	LAB 65:4
19:18-22	LAB 62:1	4:6 (LXX)	JosAsen 10:2 ftnt g
19:23	LAB 62:2	5:17-28	Eup 30:3 ftnt h
20:3	LAB 62:3	6:2	Eup 34:13 ftnt x
20:8	LAB 62:8		

2 Samuel (cont.)
7:1f.	PssSol 17:4
7:1f.	Eup 30:5 ftnt p
7:2	LivPro 17:1
7:8	Ps 151A (Heb):7
7:17	LivPro 17:1 ftnt a
8:1-14	Eup 30:3 ftnt h
8:2	Eup 33:1 ftnt b
11:2	JosAsen 23:1 ftnt b
11:2-4	LivPro 17:2
11:14-17	LivPro 17:3
12:22	JosAsen 11:12 ftnt i2
12:24	JosAsen 21:9 ftnt r
12:26-31	Eup 33:1 ftnt b
13:34	JosAsen 14:9 ftnt o
21:15-22	LAB 61:6
22:43	JosAsen 13:7 ftnt d
23:10	LAB 27:11
23:13-17	4Mac 3:7
23:15	4Mac 3:6 ftnt b
24:1f.	Eup 30:5 ftnt n
24:16	PssSol 2:22 ftnt s

1 Kings
1:48	JosAsen 3:3 ftnt f
2:12 (LXX)	Eup 30:8 ftnt t
3:1	Eup 34:10
3:1f.	HelSynPr 6:8
3:4f.	Eup 34:12 ftnt w
3:9	LAB 21:2
3:9	PrJac 1:17 ftnt h2
4:20	JosAsen 20:8 ftnt q
4:38f.	AscenIs 2:10
5:2-6	Eup 31:1 ftnt a
5:9 (LXX)	PrJac 1:17 ftnt h2
5:11	Eup 31:1 ftnt c
5:15	Eup 30:4 ftnt l
5:17-32	Eup 34:2 ftnt d
5:21	JosAsen 3:3 ftnt f
5:25	Eup 33:1 ftnt c
5:25f.	Eup 34:16 ftnt a2
5:27-28	Eup 34:2 ftnt f
5:28-29	Eup 32:1 ftnt b
6:1	Eup 34:2 ftnt e
6:1–ch. 7	Eup 34:2
6:2	Eup 34:2 ftnt g
6:5	LivPro 12:12 ftnt f
6:15	Eup 34:3
6:15	Eup 34:4 ftnt l
6:15	Eup 34:3
6:18	Eup 34:3
6:19f.	Eup 34:3 ftnt k
6:31-35	Eup 34:6
6:36	Eup 34:3 ftnt i
7:1-12	Eup 34:10
7:12	Eup 34:3 ftnt i
7:13f.	Eup 34:1 ftnt a
7:15-22	Eup 34:4 ftnt n
7:17	Eup 34:9 ftnt s
7:23-39	Eup 34:7 ftnt r
7:27	Eup 34:9 ftnt u
7:31 (LXX)	Eup 34:7 ftnt q
7:40 (LXX)	Eup 34:7 ftnt q
7:49	Eup 34:5 ftnt p
8:1f.	HelSynPr 6:8
8:3f.	Eup 34:13 ftnt x
8:5	Eup 34:13
8:15	JosAsen 3:3 ftnt f
8:27-29	3Mac 2:16
8:29	Jub 22:29
8:33-53	3Mac 2:10
8:46	LAB 19:9
8:46	HelSynPr 11:10
8:47	JosAsen 12:4 ftnt r
8:52	Jub 22:29
8:53	Jub 2:19
9:26-28	Eup 30:7 ftnt s
10:9	JosAsen 3:3 ftnt f
10:16f.	Eup 34.20 ftnt b
11:29	LivPro 5:2 ftnt c
11:29	LivPro 18:1
11:31-33	LivPro 18:1
11:42	Eup 34.20 ftnt c
12:11	JosAsen 11:18 ftnt s2
12:14	JosAsen 11:18 ftnt s2
12:15	Jub 26:18
12:28	LivPro 18:4
13:1-32	LivPro 19:1
14:7-14	LivPro 18:3
14:11	JosAsen 10:13 ftnt y
17:1	AscenIs 2:13
17:1	LAB 48:1
17:1	LivPro 21:1
17:1	LivPro 21:4
17:1-7	LivPro 10:4
17:4	LAB 48:1

17:6	LivPro 21:13	13:20f.	LivPro 22:3 ftnt d
17:8-16	LivPro 10:5	13:20f.	LivPro 22:17
17:8-16	LivPro 21:6	14:9	Ah 166 ftnt m
17:17-24	LivPro 10:6	16:18 (LXX)	LivPro 22:15 ftnt i
17:17-24	LivPro 21:7	17:1-6	AscenIs 2:15
18:1f.	HelSynPr 6:9	17:1-6	AscenIs 3:2
18:3-16	LivPro 9:3 ftnt c	17:2	Jub 1:9
18:7	LivPro 9:2	17:2-6	Dem Frag 6:1 ftnt f
18:24	LAB 38:3	17:3	Dem Frag 6:1 ftnt b
18:38 (LXX)	LivPro 21:9 ftnt j	17:15	Jub 1:9
19:8	LAE Vita 6:3	17:24-41	4Bar 8:11
19:16	LivPro 22:1	18:1–ch. 25	Dem Frag 6:1 ftnt d
21:7	LivPro 10:6	18:9	Dem Frag 6:1 ftnt b
21:20	Jub 7:23	18:9	Dem Frag 6:1 ftnt f
22:6	AscenIs 2:12	18:9-11	AscenIs 3:2
22:8	LivPro 6:2 ftnt c	18:42	JosAsen 11:1x ftnt d
22:11	AscenIs 2:12	19:1f.	HelSynPr 6:10
22:24	AscenIs 2:12	19:15	JosAsen 8:9 ftnt u
22:24-28	AscenIs 2:13	19:35	3Mac 6:5
22:52	AscenIs 2:13	20:1f.	HelSynPr 6:10
		20:2	JosAsen 11:1y ftnt h
2 Kings		20:8-11	JosAsen 16:23 ftnt h2
1:1-8	AscenIs 2:14	20:12-18	LivPro 1:13
1:1-17	LivPro 21:11	20:20	LivPro 1:5 ftnt i
1:8	AscenIs 2:10	21:6	AscenIs 2:5
1:9-12	LivPro 21:12	21:9	AscenIs 1:9
1:10	JosAsen 25:6 ftnt l	21:9	AscenIs 2:4
1:12	JosAsen 25:6 ftnt l	21:14	Jub 1:13
1:13-15	LivPro 9:3	21:14	Jub 1:19
1:14	JosAsen 25:6 ftnt l	21:16	AscenIs 2:5
2:8	LivPro 21:14	21:17	AscenIs 2:6
2:11	JosAsen 17:8 ftnt j	23:17f.	LivPro 19:2
2:11	LAE Vita 25:3	24:1f.	Eup 39:5 ftnt d
2:11	LivPro 21:15	24:1–25:21	Eup 39:2 ftnt a
2:13f.	LivPro 22:4	25:1	Dem Frag 6:1 ftnt c
2:19-22	LivPro 22:6	25:7	JosAsen 24:20 ftnt y
2:19-22	HelSynPr 6:9		
2:23f.	LivPro 22:7	*1 Chronicles*	
4:1-7	LivPro 22:8	1:17	LivPro 3:3
4:38f.	AscenIs 2:11	1:26	LivPro 3:3
4:38-41	LivPro 22:10	2:1f.	Dem Frag 2:8 ftnt b
5:1-27	LivPro 22:12	4:24	LAB 8:10 ftnt k
6:1-7	LivPro 22:11	5:4	LivPro 8:1 ftnt a
6:8-23	LivPro 22:14	5:8	LivPro 8:1 ftnt a
6:16f.	JosAsen 25:6 ftnt m	5:8	LivPro 8:1 ftnt b
9:10	PssSol 2:27 ftnt e2	6:57	LAB 45:4 ftnt e
9:24	JosAsen 27:2 ftnt d	7:13	Jub 44:30
12:9-16	LAB 29:3		

1 Chronicles (cont.)
7:21-27	LAB 15:3
8:1f.	LAB 47:11
8:7	LAB 47:11 ftnt g
8:14	LAB 47:11 ftnt g
8:20	LAB 47:11 ftnt g
8:35	LAB 47:11 ftnt g
10:12	JosAsen 10:17 ftnt h2
11:15-19	4Mac 3:7
14:8-17	Eup 30:3 ftnt h
15:29	JosAsen 7:2 ftnt e
16:25 (LXX)	PhEPoet Frags 1-2
	ftnt h
16:34	LivPro 17:1 ftnt a
17:1f.	Eup 30:5 ftnt p
18:1-3	Eup 30:5 ftnt n
21:1f.	HelSynPr 6:8
21:15	PssSol 2:22 ftnt s
22:1f.	Eup 30:6 ftnt q
22:5	Eup 30:8 ftnt t
22:8	Eup 30:5 ftnt o
27:32	Ah 1 ftnt b
28:1f.	Eup 30:6 ftnt q
29:1	Eup 30:8 ftnt t
29:2 (LXX)	JosAsen 2:2 ftnt c
29:22	Eup 30:8 ftnt u

2 Chronicles
1:6	Eup 34:13
2:11	Eup 30:4 ftnt l
2:16-17	Eup 32:1 ftnt b
3:1	PhEPoet Frags 1-2
	ftnt a
3:1–ch. 5	Eup 34:2
3:2	Eup 34:2 ftnt e
3:5	Eup 34:3
3:5-7	Eup 34:4 ftnt l
4:22	Eup 34:6
6:13	Eup 34:8
6:38	Jub 1:23
7:8	Jub 10:33
7:9	Jub 32:27
7:11	Eup 34:10
8:17-18	Eup 30:7 ftnt s
9:15f.	Eup 34.20 ftnt b
9:29	LivPro 19:1 ftnt a
9:30	Eup 34.20 ftnt c
10:11	JosAsen 11:18 ftnt s2

10:14	JosAsen 11:18 ftnt s2
12:11	JosAsen 1:1 ftnt b
12:12	PssSol 1:1
12:15	LivPro 19:1 ftnt a
13:4	LivPro 19:1 ftnt b
13:12	PssSol. 11:1
14:10	LivPro 20:1 ftnt a
15:1-15	LivPro 20:1
18:1f.	HelSynPr 6:10
19:7	Jub 5:16
20:7	Jub 19:9
20:29	JosAsen 28:1 ftnt a
24:6	4Mac 3:21
24:8	LAB 29:3
24:19	Jub 1:12
24:20-22	LivPro 15:6 ftnt c
24:20-22	LivPro 23:1
24:22	JosAsen 28:7 ftnt g
28:3	Jub 1:11
28:8-15	LivPro 20:2
29:2 (LXX)	JosAsen 2:2 ftnt c
31:6	Jub 32:15
32:3	LivPro 1:1 ftnt d
32:4	LivPro 1:1 ftnt d
32:30	LivPro 1:1 ftnt d
33:6	AscenIs 2:5
33:6	PrMan 10
33:6-12	PrMan 10
33:7	PrMan 10
33:9	AscenIs 1:9
33:9	AscenIs 2:4
33:10-13	HelSynPr 6:10
33:11	PrMan 9
33:11	AscenIs 3:7
33:12	PrMan 11
33:18	AscenIs 2:6
34:7	JosAsen 10:12 ftnt v
35:1f.	HelSynPr 6:10
35:8	EzekTrag 177 ftnt y2
35:13	EzekTrag 177 ftnt y2
36:1f.	Eup 39:5 ftnt d
36:5-21	Eup 39:2 ftnt a

Ezra
2:36-39	Ps-Hec Frag 4
	(1.188) ftnt d
3:2 (LXX)	LivPro 15:1
3:7	JosAsen 8:5 ftnt i

6:3	Eup 34:2 ftnt g	4:17 (LXX)	HelSynPr 2:1
7:6	Ah 1 ftnt b	4:17b-h	JosAsen 12:1 ftnt a
7:14	JosAsen 2:6 ftnt j	4:17c	JosAsen 8:9 ftnt u
8:1f.	HelSynPr 6:10	4:17k	JosAsen 10:14 ftnt a2
8:31	4Bar 5:34	4:17l-z	JosAsen 12:1 ftnt a
8:35	4Bar 9:1	4:17s	JosAsen 12:9 ftnt c2
9:5	JosAsen 10:17 ftnt i2	4:17x	JosAsen 7:1 ftnt d
9:5-15	JosAsen 12:1 ftnt a	5:1b	JosAsen 23:10 ftnt t
9:10f.	Jub 1:9	5:8	JosAsen 15:13 ftnt e2
9:12	4Bar 8:7	7:3	JosAsen 15:13 ftnt e2
10:6	JosAsen 10:1 ftnt c	8:5 (LXX)	Theod Frag 4 ftnt d
10:11	4Bar 6:16	8:5	JosAsen 15:13 ftnt e2
10:18f.	4Bar 8:3	8:15	JosAsen 5:5 ftnt k
		9:18	3Mac 6:35
		9:19-26	3Mac 6:36
Nehemiah			
1:6	Jub 22:29		
2:14	PhEPoet Frags 4-6	*Job*	
	ftnt a	1:1	JosAsen 4:7 ftnt p
3:1f.	HelSynPr 6:12	1:1	ArisEx (PrEv 9.25.1)
3:16	LivPro 1:9 ftnt m	1:1	ArisEx (AddJob) b
9:1f.	JosAsen 12:1 ftnt a	1:1-3	JosAsen 1:3 ftnt g
9:2	Jub 1:22	1:2	ArisEx (PrEv 9.25.3)
9:6	JosAsen 8:9 ftnt u	1:3	ArisEx (PrEv 9.25.2)
9:6	JosAsen 8:9 ftnt x	1:4	JosAsen 21:8 ftnt m
9:6f.	Jub 22:27	1:6-12	LAB 45:6 ftnt g
9:12	LAB 10:7	1:8	JosAsen 4:7 ftnt p
9:15	JosAsen 16:14 ftnt n	1:14f.	ArisEx (PrEv 9.25.3)
9:19	HelSynPr 12:76	1:16	ArisEx (PrEv 9.25.3)
9:26	Jub 1:12	1:16-18	JosAsen 19:1 ftnt a
10:31	Jub 50:8	1:17	ArisEx (PrEv 9.25.3)
11:10-14	Ps-Hec Frag 4	1:18f.	ArisEx (PrEv 9.25.3)
	(1.188) ftnt d	1:21	Ps-Phoc 110f.
13:3	PssSol 17:28 ftnt v	2:3	JosAsen 4:7 ftnt p
13:19	Jub 2:29	2:5	PssSol 5:6 ftnt a
13:13-29	JosAsen 7:5 ftnt k	2:7	ArisEx (PrEv 9.25.4)
13:16f.	Jub 50:8	2:11	ArisEx (PrEv 9.25.4)
13:27	4Bar 8:7	2:11	ArisEx (AddJob) e
		3:19	Ps-Phoc 110f.
Esther		5:1	PssSol 17:43
1:6	JosAsen 2:2 ftnt c	5:11	Ah 150 ftnt g
1:6	JosAsen 2:8 ftnt m	9:2	Ah 139 ftnt y
1:10	JosAsen 2:6 ftnt j	9:18 (LXX)	JosAsen 12:8 ftnt x
2:9	JosAsen 2:6 ftnt j	14:1f.	Ps-Phoc 114
3:1	LAB 58:3 ftnt c	22:12	LAE Vita 15:3
3:8	3Mac 3:2	22:29	Ah 150 ftnt g
4:3	3Mac 4:1	25:4	Ah 139 ftnt y
4:14	LAB 39:3	25:5	LAE Apoc 36:3
4:14	JosAsen 11:12 ftnt i2	26:7	HelSynPr 4:5

Job (cont.)

26:7	HelSynPr 12:17
28:24	JosAsen 6:6 ftnt r
28:25	HelSynPr 12:34
29:15	Ps-Phoc 24-25
31:32	Ps-Phoc 24-25
32:2	ArisEx (PrEv 9.25.4)
32:4	Ps-Phoc 220
32:29f.	PssSol 3:12 ftnt o
34:21f.	JosAsen 6:6 ftnt r
37:4	Jub 2:2
38:3	LAB 31:1
38:3	LAB 51:6
38:7	Jub 2:2
38:8-11	PrMan 3
38:10	HelSynPr 12:27
38:11	HelSynPr 3:10
38:38 (LXX)	HelSynPr 4:16
40:7	LAB 31:1
42:10-17	ArisEx (PrEv 9.25.4)
42:13f.	LAB 8:8
42:17	ArisEx (AddJob) a

Psalms

1:2	OdesSol 41:6
1:2	PssSol 14:2
1:2	HelSynPr 10:6
1:3	JosAsen 16:16 ftnt r
1:3	PssSol 14:3 ftnt b
1:4	OdesSol 29:10
2:1f.	PssSol 2:1 ftnt for ch. 2
2:9	PssSol 17:23
2:10	PssSol 2:32
7:2f.	JosAsen 12:7 ftnt v
7:3	JosAsen 12:9 ftnt c2
7:8-10	Ah 173
7:12b-13	Ah 191
7:16	OdesSol 5:7 ftnt f
8:1f.	PssSol 2:1 ftnt for ch. 2
8:5	JosAsen 18:9 ftnt s
10:2	PssSol 2:1
10:14	OdesSol 7:3 ftnt a
10:16 (9:37 LXX)	JosAsen 19:5 ftnt d
11:1	PssSol 17:16
11:2	Ah 126
11:6	Ah 126

11:6	JosAsen 12:11 ftnt j2
12:3f.	PssSol 12:4
14:3	PssSol 17:15
17:1f.	PssSol 2:1 ftnt for ch. 2
17:8	JosAsen 15:7 ftnt n
17:8	JosAsen 25:5 ftnt i
18:2 (LXX)	HelSynPr 4:5
18:8	Ps-Orph 35
18:9	LAB 23:10
18:27	Ah 150 ftnt g
18:33	PssSol 17:22
18:34	JosAsen 28:8 ftnt i
18:43	JosAsen 13:7 ftnt d
19:1	OdesSol 16:17
19:4	JosAsen 1:6 ftnt m
19:6	JosAsen 6:6 ftnt r
19:10	OdesSol 30:4
19:10f.	JosAsen 8:5 ftnt i
20:4 (LXX, MT 21:3)	OdesSol 9:8
21:11	OdesSol 5:8 ftnt g
22:9	OdesSol 28:2 ftnt a
22:14	JosAsen 12:9 ftnt c2
22:16	JosAsen 13:9 ftnt g
22:16	OdesSol 28:14
22:18	OdesSol 28:18
22:18	OdesSol 31:9
22:20	OdesSol 28:5 ftnt b
22:22	JosAsen 12:11 ftnt h2
23:1	PssSol 18:2
23:5	JosAsen 8:5 ftnt i
24:2	JosAsen 12:2 ftnt j
25:18	JosAsen 10:17 ftnt i2
25:76	PrMan 13
27:1	OdesSol 5:11
27:10	JosAsen 11:3 ftnt o
27:10	LAB 59:4
28:1	PssSol 5:2
29:1f.	PssSol 1:6
31:1	OdesSol 29:1
31:3f.	OdesSol 14:5 ftnt a
31:15f.	JosAsen 12:7 ftnt v
32:2	JosAsen 11:10 ftnt e2
32:4	PssSol 2:22 ftnt u
33:9	JosAsen 12:2 ftnt p
33:12	JosAsen 8:9 ftnt e2
34:10	PssSol 18:2

34:19	4Mac 18:16	63:8	JosAsen 15:7 ftnt n
35:13	PssSol 3:8	64:1-7	Ah 126
35:19	PssSol 7:1	64:7	Ah 126
36:4 (LXX)	HelSynPr 13:9	67:18 (LXX)	HelSynPr 4:15
37:4	HelSynPr 10:3	68:2	JosAsen 28:10 ftnt k
39:9	JosAsen 13:12 ftnt o	68:8f.	FrgsPoetWrks 4 ftnt i
41:2 (LXX)	HistJos C Verso 6	68:17	LAE Vita 25:3
41:9	Ah 139	68:18	OdesSol 10:3
41:10	SyrMen 215	68:29	PssSol 1:6 ftnt e
42:3	LAB 50:5	69:13	PssSol 17:21 ftnt p
43:2f.	JosAsen 10:5 ftnt o	69:16	JosAsen 12:11 ftnt j2
43:3	OdesSol 38:1 ftnt a	69:23	OdesSol 5:5
43:5	JosAsen 10:5 ftnt o	69:23-29	PssSol 4:14
45:1	OdesSol 16:2 ftnt b	71:1	OdesSol 29:1
45:1	OdesSol 26:1	71:16	PssSol 3:3 ftnt f
45:2	JosAsen 20:5 ftnt i	72:19	JosAsen 15:12 ftnt b2
47:2 (LXX)	PhEPoet Frags 1-2 ftnt h	73:15 (LXX)	HelSynPr 12:78
		74:14	PssSol 2:25 ftnt a2
48:14	OdesSol 14:4	75:2f.	PssSol 17:21 ftnt p
49:13 (RSV)	PssSol 3:12 ftnt n	75:25	JosAsen 16:14 ftnt o
49:18f.	Ps-Phoc 110f.	76:11	PssSol 17:21 ftnt p
50:3 (LXX, MT 51:1)	OdesSol 7:10	77:18	Jub 2:2
50:4	AscenIs 10:12	77:24 (LXX)	HelSynPr 12:75
51:1	PrMan 13	78:24	LAB 10:7
51:3	PrMan 12	78:25	LAE Vita 4:3
51:4	PrMan 10	78:25	LAB 19:5
51:4	PssSol 2:15	78:27	LAB 10:7
51:9	PrMan 13	78:70f.	Ps 151A (Heb):7
51:10	Jub 1:20	79:1	PssSol 2:2
51:11	LAE Vita 27:2	79:2	PssSol 4:19
51:11	PrMan 13	79:3	PssSol 2:27 ftnt e2
51:14	PrMan 15	79:3	PssSol 8:20
52:2	Ah 100 ftnt n	80:5	JosAsen 8:5 ftnt n
53:5	PssSol 4:19	80:7	PssSol 5:7
54 (55):1f.	PssSol 1:1 ftnt a	80:19	PssSol 5:7
55:6	JosAsen 9:1 ftnt a	81:15	PssSol 3:12 ftnt n
55:12-14	Ah 139	82:6-7	LAE Vita 12:1
56:5	Ps-Phoc 124	84:10	OdesSol 4:5
57:4	Ah 100 ftnt n	85:13	Ah 9 ftnt l
57:5 (LXX; ET 58:4)	LAE Apoc 19:3 ftnt d	86:1-6	PssSol 5:10
61:2	LAB 59:4	86:15	JosAsen 11:10 ftnt d2
61:3 (LXX)	JosAsen 12:8 ftnt y	87:6	JosAsen 15:4 ftnt g
61:5	JosAsen 15:7 ftnt n	88:10 (LXX)	JosAsen 12:8 ftnt x
61:8	PrMan 15	88 (89):35	PssSol 2:8 ftnt j
62:10	Ah 137	89:5-7	PssSol 17:43
62:12	JosAsen 28:3 ftnt c	89:7	JosAsen 16:14 ftnt o
63:6	PssSol 3:3 ftnt f	89:20	Pa 151A (Heb):7

Psalms (cont.)

90:10	Jub 23:13
90:10	Jub 23:15
90:12	LAE Vita 27:3 ftnt c
90:17	PssSol 6:2
91:9	JosAsen 12:13 ftnt n2
92:12f.	JosAsen 18:9 ftnt w
92:13	PssSol 14:3
92:13-15	JosAsen 16:16 ftnt r
94:21	LAB 32:14 ftnt n
95:4 (LXX)	PhEPoet Frag 1-2 ftnt l
95:11 (LXX)	JosAsen 8:9 ftnt f2
95:11	OdesSol 11:12 ftnt n
96:7f.	PssSol 1:6
98:1	PssSol 13:1
99:6	LAB 51:6
100:3 (LXX, MT Ketib)	OdesSol 7:12
101:7	PssSol 17:27
102:1	JosAsen 11:11 ftnt h2
102:1 (LXX)	JosAsen 12:8 ftnt y
102:27	LadJac 7:35
103:2 (LXX)	HelSynPr 3:3
103:2 (LXX)	HelSynPr 12:16
103:8	PrMan 7
103:9	PrMan 13
103:24 (LXX)	HelSynPr 4:7
103:25 (LXX)	HelSynPr 12:24
103:25-26 (LXX)	HelSynPr 3:11
104:2	OdesSol 11:11 ftnt m
104:3	LAE Vita 25:3
104:4	Jub 2:2
104:7	Jub 2:2
104:7	PssSol 17:25
104:7-9	PrMan 3
104:14f.	JosAsen 8:5 ftnt i
105:1f.	LAB 19:5
105:1f.	3Mac 2:1
105:1f.	3Mac 6:2
105:40	JosAsen 16:14 ftnt n
106:1f.	3Mac 2:1
106:1f.	3Mac 6:2
106:2	OdesSol 26:11
106:6	JosAsen 12:4 ftnt r
106:9-11	EzekTrag 192 ftnt d3
106:28	Jub 22:17
106:34 (LXX)	HelSynPr 12:61
106:41	Jub 1:19
107:5f.	PssSol 5:8
107:14	JosAsen 15:12 ftnt a2
107:16	OdesSol 17:10
107:32	HelSynPr 4:12 ftnt c
107:32	LAB 11:8
109:6-15	PssSol 4:14
110:2	OdesSol 29:8 ftnt e
112:5f. (LXX)	HelSynPr 9:8
113:12 (LXX)	JosAsen 2:3 ftnt f
115:2	3Mac 6:11
115:4	JosAsen 2:3 ftnt f
116:15	LAB 40:4
116:16	OdesSol 29:11
119:7	PssSol 2:15
119:12	HelSynPr 10:6
119:103	JosAsen 8:5 ftnt i
119:145	OdesSol 26:4
120:2	PssSol 12:1
120:7	JosAsen 26:2 ftnt d
120:8 (LXX)	HelSynPr 13:12
121:1	PssSol 3:5
121:8	PssSol 4:14
121:8	HelSynPr 10:11
123:1	PssSol 3:5
123:2	OdesSol 14:1
128:3	LAB 50:1
129:3f. (LXX)	HelSynPr 11:11
131:1	Ah 136
132:2	JosAsen 8:9 ftnt w
132:4	PssSol 4:15 ftnt k
132:5	JosAsen 8:9 ftnt w
135:17	Jub 12:3
136:6	JosAsen 12:2 ftnt j
137:3f.	4Bar 7:34
138:7	JosAsen 6:5 ftnt o
139:4 (LXX; ET 140:3)	LAE Apoc 19:3 ftnt d
139:8f.	Jub 24:31
141:3	Ah 98
141:9	PssSol 4:23
142:3	JosAsen 11:11 ftnt h2
142:6	JosAsen 11:3 ftnt l
142:6f.	JosAsen 12:7 ftnt v
143:4 (LXX)	JosAsen 12:8 ftnt y
144:3 (LXX)	HelSynPr 4:25
144:18 (LXX)	HelSynPr 6:3

145:1f.	PrMan 15
145:5	PrMan 5
145:8	PrMan 7
145:13	PssSol 17:3
145:15	PssSol 5:10
146:4 (LXX)	HelSynPr 4:19
146:5 (LXX)	HelSynPr 4:1
146:10	JosAsen 19:5 ftnt d
147:4	Ah 116 ftnt g
147:6	JosAsen 6:8 ftnt t
148:5	JosAsen 12:2 ftnt p
150:3-5	LAB 21:8
151 (LXX)	LAB 62:5
151:1f.	JosAsen 21:10 ftnt s

Proverbs

1:7	SyrMen 395
1:20f.	OdesSol 33:5 ftnt e
3:18	4Mac 18:16
3:18	PssSol 14:3 ftnt b
3:27f.	Ps-Phoc 22
3:28	Ps-Phoc 117 ftnt a
3:34	JosAsen 6:8 ftnt t
3:34	Ah 150 ftnt g
4:20-22	Ah 100 ftnt m
4:25f.	SyrMen 243
5:15-17	SyrMen 241
5:20	SyrMen 240
6:1-5	Ah 130
6:6-8	Ps-Phoc 170 ftnt i
6:8a-c (LXX)	Ps-Phoc 174 ftnt j
6:9-11	SyrMen 67
6:20	SyrMen 20
6:24f.	PssSol 16:7
7:6	JosAsen 7:2 ftnt e
7:11	SyrMen 45
8:1-4	OdesSol 33:5 ftnt e
8:22	HelSynPr 5:3
8:22f.	OdesSol 41:9 ftnt h
8:22-31	Ah 94
8:22-31	Aristob Frag 5:11
9:1	JosAsen 17:6 ftnt e
9:10	SyrMen 395
9:13	JosAsen 6:3 ftnt j
9:17	SyrMen 241
10:1	SyrMen 27
10:1	SyrMen 34
10:4	SyrMen 72

10:5	SyrMen 67
10:14	SyrMen 308
10:16	SyrMen 146
10:27	SyrMen 395
10:32	Ah 156
10:40	SyrMen 70
11:1	Ps-Phoc 12f.
11:11	Ah 168
11:13	Ps-Phoc 48
11:21	Ah 174 ftnt d
11:25	Ps-Phoc 50 ftnt b
11:30	PssSol 14:3 ftnt b
12:7	Ah 174 ftnt d
12:11	Ah 127
12:18b	Ah 100 ftnt m
12:27	SyrMen 70
12:27	SyrMen 72
13:1	PssSol 18:4 ftnt d
13:3	SyrMen 308
13:4	SyrMen 70
13:4	SyrMen 72
13:12	PssSol 14:3 ftnt b
13:17	Ah 100 ftnt m
13:24	Ah 81
14:11	Ah 168
14:11	Ah 174 ftnt d
14:15	Ps-Phoc 79
14:20	SyrMen 282
14:27	SyrMen 396
14:35	Ah 102 ftnt q
15:1	Ps-Phoc 57
15:1	Ps-Phoc 64 ftnt a
15:4	PssSol 14:3 ftnt b
15:29	SyrMen 125
16:8	PssSol 5:16
16:11	Ps-Phoc 12f.
16:14	Ah 101
16:31	Ps-Phoc 229
17:15	Ps-Phoc 11
17:22	SyrMen 432
17:22	SyrMen 433
17:27	SyrMen 312
17:28	SyrMen 313
18:16	SyrMen 284
19:4	SyrMen 282
19:4	SyrMen 284
19:6	SyrMen 284
19:12	Ah 102 ftnt q

Proverbs (cont.)

19:15	SyrMen 70
19:18	Ah 81
19:26	SyrMen 82
19:26	SyrMen 87
20:2	Ah 102 ftnt q
20:3	SyrMen 75
20:3	SyrMen 139
20:3	SyrMen 176
20:10	Ps-Phoc 12f.
20:13	SyrMen 67
20:13	SyrMen 70
20:13	SyrMen 72
20:20	Ah 138
20:20	SyrMen 22
21:3	Ps-Phoc 6f.
21:7	Ah 174 ftnt d
21:12	Ah 174 ftnt d
21:16	SyrMen 173
21:23	Ps-Phoc 19-21
21:25	Ah 140 ftnt b2
21:28	Ps-Phoc 12f.
21:28	PssSol 18:4 ftnt d
22:1	SyrMen 403
22:4	SyrMen 395
22:15	Ah 81
22:22	Ps-Phoc 10 ftnt b
23:1-8	SyrMen 286
23:13f.	Ah 81
23:22	SyrMen 94
23:22	SyrMen 97
23:22-25	Ps-Phoc 6f.
23:25	SyrMen 97
24:5	Ps-Phoc 130
24:12	JosAsen 12:1 ftnt c
24:12	JosAsen 28:3 ftnt c
24:16	SyrMen 108
24:21 (LXX)	SyrMen 9
24:33f.	SyrMen 67
25:9b–10a	Ah 141
25:15b	Ah 106
25:26a	SyrMen 241
26:2	Ah 98 ftnt g
26:3	Ah 83
26:17	SyrMen 133
26:17	SyrMen 139
27:4	Ps-Phoc 64 ftnt a
27:7	Ah 188

27:20	PssSol 4:13
28:19	Ah 127
28:19	Ps-Phoc 153
29:3	SyrMen 27
29:3	SyrMen 42
29:3	SyrMen 51
29:11	Ps-Phoc 64 ftnt a
29:15	Ah 81
29:17	Ah 81
29:22	SyrMen 416
30:8	PssSol 5:16
30:10	Ps-Phoc 226
30:17	SyrMen 23
30:17	PssSol 4:20
31:6f.	Ah 189
31:20	Ps-Phoc 28f.
31:27	JosAsen 8:5 ftnt n

Ecclesiastes

1:2	HelSynPr 2:10
2:24	Ah 127
3:13	Ah 127
3:22	Ah 127
4:6	SyrMen 430
5:2	Ps-Phoc 19-21
5:15	Ps-Phoc 110f.
5:17	SyrMen 391
5:17f.	SyrMen 369
5:18	SyrMen 392
5:18f.	Ah 127
6:10b	Ah 104
7:1	SyrMen 403
7:9	Ps-Phoc 57
7:24	OdesSol 26:8 ftnt b
8:1	SyrMen 31
8:7	Ps-Phoc 117 ftnt a
8:8	SyrMen 171
8:15	JosAsen 20:8 ftnt q
9:7-10	Ah 127
9:12	Ps-Phoc 120
9:16	Ps-Phoc 130
10:4	Ah 102 ftnt q
10:12	Ah 98 ftnt g
10:20	Ah 97
11:8	SyrMen 374
12:1-7	SyrMen 102
12:5	Jub 36:1
12:5	Ps-Phoc 112 ftnt k

12:5	SyrMen 127	14:9	PssSol 4:13
12:7	Ps-Phoc 107	14:12-15	LAE Vita 12:1
		14:13	LAE Vita 15:3
Song of Solomon		14:13	PssSol 1:5
2:9	JosAsen 7:2 ftnt e	15:10	PssSol 4:13
2:17	JosAsen 18:9 ftnt x	16:12	PssSol 4:13
4:4	JosAsen 18:9 ftnt w	19:1 (LXX)	LivPro 2:8 ftnt n
4:4	Eup 30:20 ftnt b	19:14	PssSol 8:14
4:8	Jub 8:21	19:16	JosAsen 9:1 ftnt a
4:9	Jub 27:14	21:3	PssSol 8:5
4:10	Jub 27:14	22:23	PssSol 2:19 ftnt r
4:12	Jub 27:14	24:21f.	Jub 15:32
5:13	JosAsen 18:9 ftnt r	24:23	Jub 1:28
7:5	JosAsen 18:9 ftnt w	24:23	AscenIs 4:15
8:14	JosAsen 18:9 ftnt x	25:5	LAB 16:2 ftnt d
		26:19	Ps-Phoc 104 ftnt f
Isaiah		29:16	LAB 53:13
1:10	AscenIs 3:10	30:1	PssSol 3:10
1:13 (LXX)	JosAsen 14:1 ftnt c	30:20	JosAsen 8:5 ftnt n
1:15	Jub 1:12	30:22	JosAsen 10:12 ftnt v
1:19	JosAsen 2:5 ftnt i	31:7	JosAsen 10:12 ftnt v
2:2-4	PssSol 17:31 ftnt x	32:2	LAB 16:2 ftnt d
2:20	JosAsen 10:12 ftnt v	33:5	PssSol 18:10
3:24	PssSol 2:20	35:6	4Mac 10:21
5:14	PssSol 4:13	35:10	HelSynPr 16:4
6:1	AscenIs 3:10	35:10	HelSynPr 16:14
6:1	PssSol 2:5 ftnt g	37:16	JosAsen 8:9 ftnt u
6:2	LadJac 2:15	38:8	PssSol 18:12
6:2	HelSynPr 12:82	39:7	LivPro 4:1 ftnt a
6:3	4Bar 9:3	40:1–ch. 66	PssSol ftnt for ch. 11
6:3	HelSynPr 4:10	40:3	PssSol 8:17
6:3	HelSynPr 12:84	40:4	PssSol. 11:4
6:3 (LXX)	HelSynPr 4:10 ftnt b	40:6	LAE Vita 10:2
6:5	LAE Vita 6:2	40:15	LAB 7:3
6:11	PssSol 2:14 ftnt o	40:15 (LXX)	LAB 7:3 ftnt a
7:14	LAB 43:1	40:15	LAB 12:4
7:14 (LXX)	LivPro 2:8 ftnt n	40:22	HelSynPr 3:5
8:6	LivPro 1:1 ftnt d	40:22	HelSynPr 12:16
8:20 (LXX)	HelSynPr 12:69	40:26	Ah 116 ftnt g
9:5 (LXX)	HelSynPr 12:10	41:8	Jub 2:20
9:5	JosAsen 3:4 ftnt h	41:8	Jub 19:9
10:5-11	PssSol 2:24	42:1	AscenIs 8:8
10:15	Ah 104	42:1-4	PssSol 12:6
10:19-23	OdesSol 11:22 ftnt z	42:1-4	PssSol 17:21
11:2	PssSol 17:37	42:7	JosAsen 4:10 ftnt x
11:4	PssSol 17:36	42:7	JosAsen 15:12 ftnt a2
11:4	AscenIs 4:18	43:2	4Mac 18:14
11:9	OdesSol 6:8 ftnt b	44:1	Jub 2:20

Isaiah (cont.)

45:2	OdesSol 17:10
45:5	Ps-Orph 16
45:5	Aristob Frag 4:5
45:5	HelSynPr 4:27
46:6-7	FrgsPoetWrks 5 ftnt g
46:7	Jub 12:5
47:8 (LXX)	JosAsen 11:13 ftnt k2
48:13	JosAsen 12:2 ftnt p
49:1-6	PssSol 12:6
49:1-6	PssSol 17:21
49:6	PssSol 17:28
49:7	JosAsen 27:10 ftnt l
49:9	JosAsen 4:10 ftnt x
49:24	PssSol 5:3
49:26	JosAsen 8:9 ftnt w
49:26	JosAsen 27:10 ftnt l
50:4-9	PssSol 12:6
50:4-9	PssSol 17:21
50:6	PssSol 10:2
51:1f.	LAB 23:4
51:4	LAB 51:4
51:4	LAB 51:4
51:4	LAB 51:6
51:12	LAE Vita 10:2
51:17-23	PssSol 8:14
52:1	PssSol 11:7
52:7	PssSol 11:1
52:11	Jub 22:16
52:13 (LXX)	AscenIs 4:21
52:13–53:12	PssSol 12:6
52:13–53:12	PssSol 17:21
53:7	LAB 30:5
53:7-12	4Mac 10:18
53:12	PssSol 16:2
54:1	PssSol 1:3
54:5	JosAsen 27:10 ftnt l
54:8	JosAsen 27:10 ftnt l
54:15	JosAsen 15:7 ftnt l
55:5	PssSol 17:31
56:3	LAB 50:1
56:6	JosAsen 15:7 ftnt p
57:15	PssSol 18:10
57:18	PssSol 15:3
58:1	LAE Apoc 22:1
58:1	PssSol 3:3 ftnt f
58:7	Ps-Phoc 24-25
58:8	OdesSol 8:19 ftnt i
58:8	OdesSol 20:9 ftnt f
58:11	JosAsen 16:16 ftnt t
58:11 (LXX)	JosAsen 24:19 ftnt x
58:13	Jub 2:29
60:7	PssSol 2:5 ftnt g
60:16	JosAsen 8:9 ftnt w
61:3	PssSol 14:3
61:10	LAE Apoc 20:2
62:4f.	JosAsen 15:7 ftnt l
62:6	PssSol 3:3 ftnt f
63:9	Jub 1:29
63:16	3Mac 2:21
63:18	PssSol 2:2
64:1	LAB 15:6
64:4	LAB 26:13
65:14	PssSol 3:2
65:15	Jub 20:6
65:17	Jub 1:29
65:20	Jub 23:28
66:1	PssSol 2:19 ftnt r
66:1	FrgsPoetWrks 8 ftnt b
66:1	Ps-Orph 33
66:1	Aristob Frag 4:5
66:1 (LXX)	JosAsen 22:13 ftnt r
66:8	PssSol 2:8 ftnt j
66:14	JosAsen 16:16 ftnt t
66:15	LAE Vita 25:2
66:22	Jub 1:29

Jeremiah

1:1	LivPro 2:1
1:6	LAB 56:6
1:6-9	Ah 114
1:17	LAB 51:6
1:18	4Bar 1:1
2:8	LAB 30:4
2:12	PssSol 2:9
2:13	JosAsen 2:12 ftnt r
4:8	HistRech 8:6 ftnt n
4:11-13	PssSol 8:2
4:13	LAE Vita 25:2
4:19	PssSol 2:14 ftnt o
4:31	LAB 12:5 ftnt e
5:22	HelSynPr 12:27
6:25	Jub 22:8
7:9	LAB 44:6 ftnt c
7:15	PssSol 2:4

7:33	PssSol 4:19 ftnt n	38 (31):35 (LXX)	JosAsen 12:2 ftnt f
8:1f.	PssSol 4:19 ftnt n	40:1-7	4Bar 4:6
8:2	Jub 23:23	43:6f.	4Bar 3:15
8:6	JosAsen 9:2 ftnt c	43:6f.	4Bar 4:6
9:3-6	Ah 139	43:6f.	4Bar 4:12
9:22	Ah 207	43:7	LivPro 2:1 ftnt a
9:23	Ps-Phoc 53 ftnt c	43:8	LivPro 2:2
10:3	Jub 12:5	43:9	LivPro 2:2
10:9	Jub 12:5	43:13	JosAsen 1:2 ftnt e
10:23	Ah 122	44:30–51:30 (LXX)	Eup 30:4 ftnt m
11:17	Jub 7:34	45:2-5	4Bar 7:25
12:6	Ah 139	46:15 (LXX 26:15)	LivPro 2:8 ftnt n
16:4	Ps-Phoc 99	47:4	Jub 8:21
16:13	PssSol 9:1	48:23	LivPro 8:1 ftnt b
17:8	JosAsen 16:16 ftnt r	51:34	PssSol 2:25
17:21	Jub 2:29	51:34 (LXX 28:32)	PssSol 2:25 ftnt a2
17:22f.	Ah 175 ftnt e	52:17-19	4Bar 3:18
17:27	Jub 2:29	52:27-30	4Bar 4:6
18:8	Jub 5:17		
20:11	OdesSol 5:4 ftnt c	*Lamentations*	
21:8	JosAsen 24:7 ftnt e2	1:18	PssSol 2:15 ftnt p
22:19	Ps-Phoc 99	1:20	PssSol 2:14 ftnt o
22:19	PssSol 2:27 ftnt e2	4:20 (LXX)	PssSol 17:32 ftnt z
22:26	PssSol 9:1		
23:5	PssSol 17:32	*Ezekiel*	
23:9	PssSol 8:5	1:1	LivPro 3:5
24:7	Jub 1:18	1:1f.	LAE Vita 25:2
25:4	Jub 1:12	1:3	LivPro 3:1
25:11f.	Dem Frag 6:1 ftnt f	1:27	LAE Vita 25:3
26:1f.	Eup 39:3 ftnt b	1:28	PssSol 2:5 ftnt g
27 (50):5	JosAsen 15:7 ftnt l	2:1	JosAsen 14:8 ftnt m
29:10	Dem Frag 6:1 ftnt f	3:18	LAB 37:2
29:13	Jub 1:15	4:14	PssSol 8:12
29:14	Jub 1:15	5:11	PssSol 1:8 ftnt g
29:18	Jub 20:6	5:16	PssSol 2:24 ftnt w
31:2-9	Ah 175 ftnt e	6:5	PssSol 4:19 ftnt n
31:9	Jub 1:24	8:1	LAB 28:6
31:9	Jub 2:20	8:3	LivPro 3:14
31:33	LAE Apoc 13:5	9:3	LadJac 5:7 ftnt d
32:41	Jub 1:15	9:6	Jub 23:23
33:18 (LXX)	LivPro 6:1 ftnt a	10:1f.	LAE Vita 25:2
35:1f.	HistRech 8:1a	10:4	LadJac 5:7 ftnt d
35:6-11	HistRech 8:3	10:18	PssSol 1:8 ftnt g
35:6f.	HistRech 9:8	10:18f.	LadJac 5:7 ftnt d
35:12-19	HistRech 10:2 ftnt d	11:22f.	LadJac 5:7 ftnt d
36:1f.	Eup 39:3 ftnt b	13:11	Ah 169
36:3	Jub 5:17	14:13-23	PssSol 13:3
38:4-13	4Bar 3:13	16:38	PssSol 2:24 ftnt w

Ezekiel (cont.)
16:40	Jub 20:4
16:41	PssSol 2:24 ftnt w
18:7	Ps-Phoc 12f.
18:31	LAE Apoc 13:5
20:1f.	LAB 28:6
20:12	Jub 2:21
20:12	Jub 2:19
20:28	Jub 1:10
20:31	Jub 1:11
23:38	PssSol 1:8 ftnt g
24:7	Jub 7:30
27:13	Jub 9:10
28:5	Ah 137
29:3	PssSol 2:25 ftnt a2
29:5	PssSol 4:19 ftnt n
31:8f.	JosAsen 18:9 ftnt w
32:2	PssSol 2:25 ftnt a2
33:1-6	LAE Apoc 22:2
33:11	HelSynPr 11:6
36:26	LAE Apoc 13:5
37:1-6	OdesSol 22:9
37:1-14	LivPro 3:12
37:3	4Mac 18:18
38:12	Jub 8:12
38:12	Jub 8:19
38:12	PrJac 1:8 ftnt i
38:19	PssSol 2:24 ftnt w
38:20	Jub 23:19
38:22	FrgsPoetWrks 6 ftnt d
39:17	PssSol 4:19 ftnt n
40:1–ch. 42	LivPro 3:15
44:9	PssSol 17:28 ftnt v
45:8	PssSol 17:28
45:10	Ps-Phoc 12f.
45:18	EzekTrag 177 ftnt y2
47:1-12	OdesSol 6:8 ftnt b
47:5	PhEPoet Frags 4-6 ftnt f
47:8-11	4Bar 9:18
47:13	PssSol 17:28
47:21	PssSol 17:28
47:22f.	PssSol 17:28 ftnt v

Daniel
1:3	LivPro 4:1
1:6	LivPro 4:1 ftnt a
1:7	LivPro 4:15

2:22	LAB 22:3
2:22	HelSynPr 9:6
2:28 (LXX)	LivPro 2:8 ftnt m
3:1f.	LAB 6:5f. ftnt d
3:1f.	LAB 6:16
3:1f.	LAB 38:1 ftnt b
3:1f.	4Mac 13:9
3:1f.	4Mac 16:3
3:1f.	4Mac 16:21
3:1f.	4Mac 18:12
3:1f.	HelSynPr 4:24
3:1f.	HelSynPr 6:11
3:15	Ah 123 ftnt n
3:24-45	JosAsen 12:1 ftnt a
3:27	3Mac 6:6
3:29	JosAsen 12:4 ftnt r
3:50	3Mac 6:6
4:7-9	Ah 175 ftnt e
4:8	JosAsen 21:21 ftnt b2
4:13	Jub 4:15
4:13 (LXX Theodotion)	JosAsen 10:16 ftnt e2
4:17-19	Ah 175 ftnt e
4:29 (32)	LivPro 4:13
4:30 (33)	LivPro 4:4
4:31f. (34f.)	LivPro 4:13
4:33a-b (LXX)	JosAsen 10:17 ftnt h2
4:33a-34 (LXX)	JosAsen 10:1 ftnt b
4:34 (LXX)	JosAsen 12:1 ftnt a
5:1 (LXX)	LivPro 4:15 ftnt j
5:12	LivPro 4:15
6:1f.	4Mac 16:3
6:1f.	4Mac 16:21
6:1f.	4Mac 18:12
6:1f.	HelSynPr 4:24
6:1f.	HelSynPr 6:11
6:4	JosAsen 4:7 ftnt p
6:11	JosAsen 11:1y ftnt i
6:11	JosAsen 11:19 ftnt t2
6:24	3Mac 6:7
7:1f.	EzekTrag 70 ftnt b2
7:9 (Theodotian)	JosAsen 5:4 ftnt g
7:10	AscenIs 9:22
7:10	JosAsen 16:17 ftnt a2
7:10	HelSynPr 12:83
7:13-14	EzekTrag 67 ftnt z
7:15 (LXX)	JosAsen 12:8 ftnt y
8:10	LAE Vita 15:3

8:11	PrJos Frag A	5:26	Jub 12:5
8:13 (Theodotion)	HelSynPr 4:8	8:4	Ps-Phoc 19-21
8:13	HelSynPr 4:8 ftnt a	8:4-6	Ps-Phoc 12f.
8:15	JosAsen 1:1 ftnt b	9:2-4	Jub 24:31
8:17f.	JosAsen 14:3 ftnt g	9:7	Jub 8:21
9:4-19	JosAsen 12:1 ftnt a	9:7	Jub 24:30
9:5 (Theodotion)	JosAsen 12:4 ftnt r	9:15	Jub 7:34
9:18	Jub 22:29		
9:24-27	Dem Frag 6:1 ftnt f	*Obadiah*	
10:3	JosAsen 8:5 ftnt i	4	LAE Vita 15:3
10:6	JosAsen 14:9 ftnt q		
10:13	Jub 15:32	*Jonah*	
11:11f.	3Mac 1:1	1:3	LivPro 10:6
11:30	Jub 23:16	1:17–2:9	3Mac 6:8
11:30	Jub 24:29	2:1f.	HelSynPr 4:24
11:31	PrMan 10 ftnt r2	2:1f.	HelSynPr 6:11
12:2	JosAsen 8:9 ftnt g2	2:11 (10)	LivPro 10:2
12:2	LAB 33:5 ftnt e	3:1-5	LivPro 10:2
12:2	Ps-Phoc 104 ftnt f	3:1f.	HelSynPr 11:7
12:2	PssSol 3:12 ftnt o	3:4	LivPro 10:3
		3:10	LivPro 10:3
Hosea			
1:8	PrJos Frag A ftnt a	*Micah*	
1:10	Jub 1:24	1:1	LivPro 6:1
2:1	JosAsen 19:8 ftnt h	1:4	JosAsen 28:10 ftnt k
2:24	PrJos Frag A ftnt a	6:11	Ps-Phoc 12f.
4:3	Jub 23:18	7:1	LadJac 7:28
8:1	LAE Apoc 22:2	7:6	Ah 139
8:8 (LXX)	LAE Apoc 26:1 ftnt b	7:10	JosAsen 13:7 ftnt d
9:4	JosAsen 8:5 ftnt n		
10:1	JosAsen 2:5 ftnt i	*Nahum*	
12:3f.	PrJos Frag A	1:1	LivPro 11:1 ftnt a
12:8	Ps-Phoc 12f.	1:5f.	PrMan 4
14:2	PssSol 15:3		
14:2	OdesSol 8:2 ftnt b	*Habakkuk*	
		2:11	LivPro 10:11
Joel		2:14	OdesSol 6:8 ftnt b
1:1f.	LivPro 8:1		
2:10	LAE Apoc 36:3	*Zephaniah*	
2:13	PrMan 7	1:3	Jub 23:19
2:13	HelSynPr 2:3	1:4	LivPro 13:1
3:15	LAE Apoc 36:3	1:12	LivPro 13:1
4:6	PssSol 2:3 ftnt d	2:1-15	LivPro 13:2
4:7	PssSol 2:25 ftnt z	3:2	LAE Vita 12:1
4:17	PssSol 17:28 ftnt v		
		Haggai	
		1:13	LivPro 14:1
Amos		1:14	LivPro 14:2
1:14	Ah 169		

Zechariah		14:8	OdesSol 6:8 ftnt b
1:1	LivPro 15:6 ftnt c		
1:12	Dem Frag 6:1 ftnt f	*Malachi*	
2:12	LAB 19:10 ftnt m	1:1 (LXX)	LivPro 16:2
2:15 (LXX)	JosAsen 15:7 ftnt l	1:2f.	LAB 32:5
5:1-3 (LXX)	LivPro 3:5	1:11	OdesSol 10:5 ftnt c
5:1f.	OdesSol 23:5 ftnt c	1:11	HelSynPr 2:7
8:3	JosAsen 15:7 ftnt l	1:11	HelSynPr 2:7
8:13	Jub 1:16	2:3	LAE Apoc 6:2
8:19	LAB 19:7	3:2	4Mac 9:22
9:3	JosAsen 13:7 ftnt d	3:19	FrgsPoetWrks 6 ftnt d
9:12	LivPro 15:6	3:20	JosAsen 6:2 ftnt i
13:4	AscenIs 2:10	3:24	LAB 23:13
13:6 (LXX)	LadJac 7:30	4:6	LAB 23:13
14:1f.	PssSol 17:21 ftnt p		

NEW TESTAMENT

Matthew		14:19f.	4Bar 9:21
1:18-21	AscenIs 11:3	16:14	LivPro 2:19 ftnt z
1:18f.	JosAsen 21:1 ftnt b	16:17	JosAsen 16:8 ftnt f
1:25	JosAsen 21:1 ftnt a	16:18	JosAsen 15:7 ftnt l
2:2	Aristob Frag 4:5	16:18	OdesSol 22:12
2:2	Ps-Orph 31	17:2	JosAsen 18:9 ftnt p
2:13-15	LivPro 2:8 ftnt n	18:10	PrJos Frag A
3:4	AscenIs 2:10	19:17	HelSynPr 9:5
4:2	LAE Vita 6:3	22:2	JosAsen 20:8 ftnt r
5:1-12	JosAsen 21:10 ftnt s	22:4	JosAsen 10:13 ftnt x
5:6	4Bar 9:21	22:11	JosAsen 20:6 ftnt n
5:13	JosAsen 11:4 ftnt q	22:32	HelSynPr 16:8
5:16	JosAsen 20:7 ftnt p	22:32	HelSynPr 16:14 ftnt d
5:18	LAB 11:5 ftnt e	23:11f.	Ah 150 ftnt g
5:25f.	Ah 142	23:12	JosAsen 6:8 ftnt t
5:43-48	JosAsen 29:5 ftnt c	23:35	LivPro 23:1
6:13	OdesSol 14:5	23:35	LivPro 15:6 ftnt c
6:19-21 par	JosAsen 12:15 ftnt q2	23:35-36	LAB 6:11 ftnt j
6:23	JosAsen 6:6 ftnt r	24:6	LivPro 2:8 ftnt m
7:2	Ps-Phoc 11	24:22	LAB 19:13 ftnt r
7:6	JosAsen 10:13 ftnt y	24:24	AscenIs 4:12
7:12	Ah 52 ftnt c	24:31	LAE Apoc 22:3
7:12	LAB 11:12 ftnt k	25:14-30	Ah 192
7:28	JosAsen 15:11 ftnt z	25:28f.	Ah 143 ftnt b
9:18	JosAsen 19:1 ftnt a	25:46	JosAsen 8:9 ftnt g2
9:37	JosAsen 1:2 ftnt d	26:31	AscenIs 3:14
10:20	AscenIs 1:7	26:52	JosAsen 29:4 ftnt b
10:28	4Mac 13:15	26:52	SyrMen 18-19
11:21	JosAsen 13:2 ftnt a	26:53	JosAsen 25:6 ftnt m
12:8	AscenIs 1:4	27:25	LAB 6:11 ftnt j

27:52f.	AscenIs 9:17	14:18	SyrMen 215
27:62-66	AscenIs 3:14	14:31 par	JosAsen 24:11 ftnt n
27:63	LAB 11:2 ftnt c	14:32-42 par	JosAsen 14:4 ftnt i
28:3	JosAsen 5:4 ftnt g	14:35 par	JosAsen 11:19 ftnt t2
28:3	JosAsen 14:9 ftnt q	14:62	OdesSol 19:10 ftnt h
28:4	AscenIs 3:14		
28:8	JosAsen 9:1 ftnt a	*Luke*	
28:18-20	AscenIs 11:23	1:5	JosAsen 1:1 ftnt b
28:19	AscenIs 3:18	1:26-38	OdesSol 19:10
		1:38	OdesSol 29:11
Mark		1:48	JosAsen 11:12 ftnt j2
1:6	AscenIs 2:10	1:52	JosAsen 6:8 ftnt t
1:10	JosAsen 14:2 ftnt e	1:52	Ah 150 ftnt g
1:11	AscenIs 1:4	1:59	JosAsen 1:1 ftnt b
1:11	OdesSol 7:15	2:7-16	LivPro 2:8 ftnt n
1:17 par	JosAsen 21:21 ftnt c2	2:11	PssSol 17:32 ftnt z
1:24	PrJos Frag A ftnt m	2:12	LivPro 2:8 ftnt n
1:32	JosAsen 10:16 ftnt g2	2:13	JosAsen 14:8 ftnt k
2:8 par	JosAsen 23:8 ftnt q	2:15	JosAsen 17:1 ftnt a
2:8	JosAsen 26:6 ftnt j	2:19	LAE Apoc 3:3
2:15	JosAsen 20:8 ftnt q	2:25	JosAsen 4:7 ftnt p
3:16 par	JosAsen 15:7 ftnt l	2:40	JosAsen 4:7 ftnt p
3:22	Jub 10:8	2:51	LAE Apoc 3:3
4:15 par	JosAsen 12:9 ftnt c2	2:52	JosAsen 4:7 ftnt p
4:32 par	JosAsen 16:23 ftnt h2	3:36	Jub 8:2
5:35	JosAsen 19:1 ftnt a	4:13	LAE Vita 17:2
6:3 par	JosAsen 4:10 ftnt v	6:32-35	Ps-Phoc 152 ftnt i
6:13	LAE Vita 36:2 ftnt a	6:38	Ps-Phoc 12f.
6:50 par	JosAsen 14:11 ftnt s	6:41	JosAsen 11:19 ftnt t2
7:15	Ps-Phoc 228	7:5	JosAsen 10:11 ftnt u
7:27 par	JosAsen 10:13 ftnt y	7:29	PssSol 2:15 ftnt p
7:27 par	JosAsen 10:13 ftnt y	7:36-50	JosAsen 20:2 ftnt f
8:31	LAB 11:2 ftnt c	7:39	JosAsen 23:8 ftnt q
9:7	AscenIs 1:4	7:44	JosAsen 7:1 ftnt b
9:31	LAB 11:2 ftnt c	9:28	JosAsen 11:1 ftnt a
10:12	LAB 42:1 ftnt b	9:35	AscenIs 8:8
10:17-31 par	JosAsen 12:15 ftnt s2	9:51	PssSol 4:18 ftnt m
10:21 par	JosAsen 10:11 ftnt u	9:52	JosAsen 3:2 ftnt d
10:34	LAB 11:2 ftnt c	9:54	JosAsen 25:6 ftnt l
11:1 par	JosAsen 3:2 ftnt d	10:1	JosAsen 2:11 ftnt q
12:26	4Mac 7:19	10:13	JosAsen 13:2 ftnt a
12:26f.	4Mac 16:25	10:18	LAE Vita 12:1
13:11	Ah 114	10:20	JosAsen 15:4 ftnt g
13:12	JosAsen 11:3 ftnt o	10:30	JosAsen 27:3 ftnt f
13:12	Ps-Phoc 47 ftnt c	10:30-35	JosAsen 29:5 ftnt c
13:20	LAB 19:13 ftnt r	10:37	JosAsen 23:3 ftnt i
13:22	AscenIs 4:12	10:41	JosAsen 14:4 ftnt i
14:9 par	JosAsen 19:8 ftnt f	11:7	JosAsen 10:2 ftnt g

Luke (cont.)

11:7	JosAsen 10:6 ftnt q
12:11f.	Ah 114
12:13-21	Ah 137
12:19	JosAsen 20:8 ftnt q
12:20	Ps-Phoc 106 ftnt h
12:37	AscenIs 4:16
14:11	Ah 150 ftnt g
14:29f.	SyrMen 344
14:31	SyrMen 340
15:1f.	JosAsen 9:2 ftnt c
15:7	JosAsen 15:8 ftnt v
15:10	JosAsen 15:8 ftnt v
15:13	HelSynPr 11:9
15:15f.	JosAsen 3:5 ftnt i
15:18	JosAsen 7:4 ftnt i
15:19	JosAsen 6:8 ftnt t
15:19	JosAsen 11:5 ftnt r
15:19	JosAsen 12:5 ftnt t
15:20	HelSynPr 11:9
15:21	JosAsen 7:4 ftnt i
15:21	JosAsen 11:5 ftnt r
15:21	JosAsen 12:5 ftnt t
15:22	JosAsen 15:10 ftnt y
15:23	JosAsen 20:8 ftnt q
15:24	JosAsen 8:9 ftnt a2
15:24	JosAsen 11:5 ftnt r
15:24	JosAsen 19:10 ftnt l
15:32	JosAsen 8:9 ftnt a2
15:32	JosAsen 11:5 ftnt r
16:1	JosAsen 3:5 ftnt i
16:3	Ps-Phoc 158
16:21	JosAsen 10:13 ftnt y
16:23	HelSynPr 16:4
16:26	PrJac 1:11 ftnt u
18:2	JosAsen 28:7 ftnt e
18:11	JosAsen 11:19 ftnt t2
18:13	JosAsen 10:15 ftnt c2
18:13	JosAsen 11:19 ftnt t2
18:14	Ah 150 ftnt g
18:20	LAB 11:10 ftnt i
19:5	JosAsen 3:2 ftnt d
19:8	JosAsen 10:11 ftnt u
19:12-27	Ah 193
19:24-26	Ah 143 ftnt b
20:38	HelSynPr 16:8
20:38	HelSynPr 16:14 ftnt d
21:24	JosAsen 26:5 ftnt i
22:25	JosAsen 21:8 ftnt o
22:44	JosAsen 4:9 ftnt s
23:35	AscenIs 8:8
23:43	LAE Vita 25:3 ftnt a
23:46	LAE Apoc 42:8
24:4	AscenIs 3:17
24:7	LAB 11:2 ftnt c
24:38f.	JosAsen 10:5 ftnt o

John

1:1	OdesSol 41:14
1:1	HelSynPr 5:20
1:1	HelSynPr 12:10
1:1	HelSynPr 16:5
1:1	HelSynPr 16:14 ftnt d
1:1-3	OdesSol 16:7 ftnt d
1:1-4	Ah 95
1:1-18	HelSynPr 5:20 ftnt g
1:1-18	OdesSol 12:3 ftnt a
1:1-18	OdesSol 16:10 ftnt e
1:1-18	OdesSol 32:2
1:3	JosAsen 12:2 ftnt p
1:3	HelSynPr 3:1
1:3	HelSynPr 12:12
1:3	HelSynPr 12:15
1:3	HelSynPr 12:28
1:3	HelSynPr 14:1
1:4	JosAsen 12:2 ftnt q
1:4	OdesSol 3:9 ftnt d
1:5	OdesSol 18:6
1:9	4Bar 9:4
1:9	4Bar 9:20
1:10	JosAsen 12:2 ftnt p
1:11	OdesSol 7:12
1:13	JosAsen 28:11 ftnt m
1:14	OdesSol 12:12 ftnt i
1:14	PrJos Frag A
1:14	HelSynPr 1:2
1:14	HelSynPr 12:9
1:18	HelSynPr 12:9
1:18	HelSynPr 12:10
1:26	OdesSol 30:6 ftnt d
1:27	JosAsen 12:5 ftnt t
1:30	OdesSol 28:19
2:11	LivPro 1:2 ftnt c
2:25	JosAsen 23:8 ftnt q
3:5	JosAsen 8:9 ftnt g2
3:16	OdesSol 9:7

4:10	OdesSol 6:18	12:3	JosAsen 17:4 ftnt d
4:10	OdesSol 11:7	12:31	AscenIs 2:4
4:10-15	OdesSol 6:18 ftnt q	12:31	LAE Vita 12:1
4:14	OdesSol 6:18	12:35	OdesSol 18:14 ftnt i
4:14	OdesSol 10:2	12:50	JosAsen 12:2 ftnt q
5:17-26	Art Frag 3 (PrEv 9.27.23) ftnt j2	13:1-7	JosAsen 7:1 ftnt b
		13:1-17	JosAsen 20:2 ftnt f
5:21	JosAsen 20:7 ftnt p	13:13	SyrMen 366
5:24	JosAsen 8:9 ftnt a2	13:18	Ah 139
5:26	OdesSol 3:9 ftnt d	13:18	SyrMen 215
5:40	OdesSol 3:9 ftnt d	13:23	JosAsen 10:4 ftnt j
6:1f.	JosAsen 8:5 ftnt i	14:1–ch. 16	HelSynPr 7:15
6:33-37	OdesSol 41:11	14:1–ch. 16	HelSynPr 9:9
6:35	JosAsen 8:5 ftnt k	14:2	OdesSol 11:23
6:38	PrJos Frag A	14:2-3	OdesSol 3:5
6:48	JosAsen 8:5 ftnt k	14:2f.	JosAsen 15:7 ftnt u
7:14	EzekTrag 2 ftnt b	14:6	OdesSol 11:3 ftnt c
7:19	EzekTrag 12 ftnt g	14:6	OdesSol 3:9 ftnt d
7:24	Ps-Phoc 9 ftnt a	14:17	Jub 25:14
7:32 (8:32 sic)	EzekTrag 104 ftnt h2	14:17	OdesSol 3:10 ftnt f
7:37f.	OdesSol 6:18	14:19b	OdesSol 3:8
7:37f.	OdesSol 11:7	14:26	OdesSol 3:10
7:38	OdesSol 6:18 ftnt q	14:26	OdesSol 3:10 ftnt f
7:48	FrgsPoetWrks 8 ftnt b	14:30	AscenIs 2:4
8:4	JosAsen 4:10 ftnt w	15:1f.	OdesSol 17:16
8:10	OdesSol 19:10 ftnt h	15:9f.	OdesSol 8:20
8:12	OdesSol 12:3 ftnt a	15:9f.	OdesSol 8:21 ftnt k
8:12	OdesSol 18:14 ftnt i	15:26	JosAsen 19:11 ftnt m
8:32	EzekTrag 104 ftnt h2	15:26	OdesSol 3:10 ftnt f
8:44	JosAsen 12:9 ftnt b2	16:11	AscenIs 2:4
8:44	JosAsen 12:9 ftnt e2	16:20	JosAsen 11:6 ftnt u
8:57-59	OdesSol 28:19	16:30	JosAsen 13:11 ftnt k
8:58	PrJos Frag A	17:1-9	OdesSol 31:4
9:2	OdesSol 11:3 ftnt c	17:7	JosAsen 13:11 ftnt k
9:7	LivPro 1:2 ftnt g	17:11f.	OdesSol 8:21 ftnt k
9:31	JosAsen 4:7 ftnt m	17:24	OdesSol 3:5
10:7-9	OdesSol 12:3 ftnt a	17:24b	OdesSol 41:15
10:7-10	OdesSol 17:9	18:11	JosAsen 29:4 ftnt b
10:7-10	OdesSol 17:11	18:16f.	JosAsen 10:2 ftnt g
10:7-10	OdesSol 42:17	19:30	LAE Vita 45:3
10:10	OdesSol 3:9 ftnt d	19:31	AscenIs 3:13
10:14	OdesSol 8:12	20:12	AscenIs 3:17
10:17	JosAsen 15:8 ftnt w	20:22	JosAsen 19:11 ftnt m
10:28	JosAsen 12:11 ftnt l2	20:28	JosAsen 22:3 ftnt d
10:28	OdesSol 3:9 ftnt d	20:30	LivPro 1:2 ftnt e
11:10	JosAsen 6:6 ftnt r	21:15-18	JosAsen 4:3 ftnt e
11:25	OdesSol 3:9	21:15-18	JosAsen 14:4 ftnt i
11:52	OdesSol 10:5		

Acts

1:4	AscenIs 8:24
1:8f.	AscenIs 11:23
1:10	LAE Apoc 33:1
1:11f.	4Bar 9:20
2:30	AscenIs 11:2
3:13	PrMan 1
3:13	HelSynPr 15:3
3:17	JosAsen 6:7 ftnt s
4:24	JosAsen 8:9 ftnt u
5:17-26	Art Frag 3 (PrEv 9.27.23) ftnt j2
5:28	LAB 6:11 ftnt j
6:5	JosAsen 4:7 ftnt p
6:8	JosAsen 4:7 ftnt p
6:15	JosAsen 18:9 ftnt o
7:15f.	Jub 46:10
7:23	Jub 47:10
7:30	Jub 48:2
7:53	Jub 1:28
7:55	LAE Apoc 33:1
8:22	JosAsen 9:2 ftnt c
8:28	JosAsen 5:4 ftnt e
9:1	JosAsen 7:4 ftnt g
9:1-8	JosAsen 14:1 ftnt a
9:3	JosAsen 14:2 ftnt f
9:3-8	JosAsen 14:1 ftnt a
9:3-9	JosAsen 6:1 ftnt c
9:4	JosAsen 14:3 ftnt g
9:4	JosAsen 14:4 ftnt i
9:4f.	JosAsen 14:6 ftnt j
9:6	JosAsen 14:8 ftnt m
9:9	JosAsen 10:17 ftnt h2
9:10f.	JosAsen 14:6 ftnt j
9:10-12	JosAsen 19:1 ftnt a
9:10-17	JosAsen 19:1 ftnt a
9:12	JosAsen 14:1 ftnt a
9:12	JosAsen 14:9 ftnt p
9:40	JosAsen 11:19 ftnt t2
10:1f.	JosAsen 1:3 ftnt g
10:1–ch. 11	JosAsen 7:1 ftnt d
10:2	JosAsen 10:11 ftnt u
10:3-5	JosAsen 14:6 ftnt j
10:3-7	JosAsen 14:1 ftnt a
10:10-16	JosAsen 14:4 ftnt i
10:24f.	JosAsen 5:3 ftnt d
10:28	JosAsen 8:5 ftnt i
10:34f.	JosAsen 7:7 ftnt m
10:40	LAB 11:2 ftnt c
12:3-5	JosAsen 10:2 ftnt g
12:6-17	Art Frag 3 (PrEv 9.27.23) ftnt j2
12:11	JosAsen 13:11 ftnt k
12:23	LAB 44:9 ftnt g
13:18	HelSynPr 5:12
13:25	JosAsen 12:5 ftnt t
13:27	JosAsen 6:7 ftnt s
14:23	JosAsen 13:15 ftnt q
15:20	JosAsen 21:10 ftnt s
15:29	Ps-Phoc 31 ftnt d
16:17	JosAsen 8:2 ftnt f
16:23-30	Art Frag 3 (PrEv 9.27.23) ftnt j2
16:28	JosAsen 8:9 ftnt y
16:34	JosAsen 7:1 ftnt c
16:34	JosAsen 20:8 ftnt q
16:36	JosAsen 20:10 ftnt u
17:25	JosAsen 12:1 ftnt c
17:28	Aristob Frag 4:6
17:29	JosAsen 2:3 ftnt f
17:30	JosAsen 6:7 ftnt s
17:32	Ps-Phoc 104 ftnt f
18:6	LAB 6:11 ftnt j
19:18f.	JosAsen 10:12 ftnt v
19:19	Ps-Phoc 149
20:8	JosAsen 14:9 ftnt r
20:25	JosAsen 13:11 ftnt k
20:26	LAB 6:11 ftnt j
20:32	JosAsen 13:15 ftnt q
20:33	JosAsen 2:4 ftnt h
22:3	JosAsen 4:7 ftnt o
22:10	JosAsen 14:8 ftnt m
22:23	JosAsen 10:14 ftnt b2
24:14	OdesSol 11:3 ftnt c
24:22	OdesSol 11:3 ftnt c
26:16	JosAsen 14:8 ftnt l
26:18	JosAsen 8:9 ftnt y

Romans

1:3	HelSynPr 6:2
1:5	HelSynPr 11:3
1:21-25	HelSynPr 12:68
1:25	HelSynPr 12:85
1:26	Ps-Phoc 192 ftnt p
1:27	Ps-Phoc 190 ftnt n
1:29	Ps-Phoc 71

2:4	HelSynPr 11:4	4:9	4Mac 17:14
2:6	JosAsen 28:3 ftnt c	5:1	Ps-Phoc 179
2:14f.	HelSynPr 11:3	5:11	Ps-Phoc 69
2:14f.	HelSynPr 12:43	6:9-11	JosAsen 12:5 ftnt u
2:22	JosAsen 10:12 ftnt v	6:10	Ps-Phoc 69
3:4	JosAsen 25:8 ftnt o	6:17	OdesSol 3:8
4:13	HelSynPr 12:62	7:16	JosAsen 11:12 ftnt i2
4:15	Jub 33:16	8:6	HelSynPr 12:6
4:17	JosAsen 12:2 ftnt e	8:6	HelSynPr 12:12
4:17	JosAsen 20:7 ftnt p	9:24	HelSynPr 2:8
5:2	OdesSol 7:3 ftnt b	10:1f.	JosAsen 8:5 ftnt i
5:12-21	LAE Apoc 14:2	10:14-22	JosAsen 8:5 ftnt i
5:17	LAE Apoc 14:2 ftnt a	10:16	JosAsen 8:5 ftnt l
5:20	LAB 39:6 ftnt d	11:2-16	JosAsen 15:1 ftnt b
5:21	JosAsen 8:9 ftnt g2	11:14	Ps-Phoc 212
6:10	4Mac 7:19	15:4	LAB 11:2 ftnt c
7:5f.	JosAsen 12:5 ftnt u	15:50-53	AscenIs 4:18
7:6	JosAsen 8:9 ftnt b2	15:52	LAE Apoc 22:3
7:7	LAE Apoc 19:3	15:54f.	OdesSol 15:8 ftnt c
7:9	JosAsen 19:10 ftnt l	15:55	HelSynPr 5:7
7:24	JosAsen 27:10 ftnt m	16:20	JosAsen 19:11 ftnt m
8:17	JosAsen 24:14 ftnt p		
8:35	OdesSol 28:5	*2 Corinthians*	
8:38	LAE Vita 21:1 ftnt a	1:3	HelSynPr 9:8
8:38	LAE Vita 28:2	3:6	JosAsen 8:9 ftnt b2
9:23	JosAsen 21:16 ftnt w	3:18	JosAsen 18:9 ftnt o
11:30	JosAsen 12:5 ftnt u	3:18	OdesSol 13:1 ftnt a
11:33	HelSynPr 4:30	4:4	AscenIs 2:4
12:4f.	OdesSol 17:16	4:6	JosAsen 14:1 ftnt c
12:17	JosAsen 23:9 ftnt s	4:18	JosAsen 12:15 ftnt q2
12:19	JosAsen 28:14 ftnt r	5:1-4	AscenIs 4:18
12:42	HelSynPr 11:3	5:1-5	LAE Apoc 31:1
13:9	LAB 11:10 ftnt i	5:19	JosAsen 11:10 ftnt e2
13:13	Ps-Phoc 69	6:15	LivPro 4:6 ftnt c
13:16-18	Ps-Phoc 69	6:16	HelSynPr 10:10
14:8	4Mac 7:19	7:1	HelSynPr 10:10
15:6	4Bar 9:14	7:15	JosAsen 9:1 ftnt a
15:8	OdesSol 31:13	11:3	LAE Apoc 14:2
16:27	Ps-Phoc 54	11:14	LAE Vita 9:1
		11:14	LAE Apoc 17:1
1 Corinthians		11:15	JosAsen 28:3 ftnt c
(1 Cor ?) 1:7	AscenIs 4:13	12:2	LAE Apoc 37:5
2:3	JosAsen 9:1 ftnt a	12:2-3	LAE Vita 25:3 ftnt a
2:3	JosAsen 15:5 ftnt i	12:4	LAE Vita 25:3 ftnt a
2:8	AscenIs 10:11		
3:1-2	OdesSol 8:14	*Galatians*	
3:6-10	OdesSol 38:17 ftnt q	2:9	JosAsen 17:6 ftnt e
4:9	JosAsen 15:5 ftnt i	2:11-14	JosAsen 7:1 ftnt d

Galatians (cont.)
2:15   Jub 23:24
2:19   4Mac 7:19
3:10   4Mac 5:20
3:19   Jub 1:28
4:26   4Bar 5:35
5:19-21   Ps-Phoc 71

Ephesians
1:4   JosAsen 8:9 ftnt e2
1:6   AscenIs 1:4
1:18   JosAsen 6:6 ftnt r
1:18   JosAsen 21:16 ftnt w
1:21   PrJos Frag A
1:21   PssSol 2:19 ftnt r
2:2   AscenIs 2:4
2:2   4Bar 9:17
2:3   LAE Apoc 3:2
2:5   JosAsen 15:5 ftnt i
2:18   OdesSol 7:3 ftnt b
2:19   OdesSol 3:6
3:6   JosAsen 15:5 ftnt i
3:6   JosAsen 24:14 ftnt p
3:15   HelSynPr 12:2
3:16   JosAsen 21:16 ftnt w
4:9f.   PrJos Frag A
4:19   Ps-Phoc 6 ftnt b
4:25   Ps-Phoc 6f.
4:31   Ps-Phoc 64 ftnt a
5:3-5   Ps-Phoc 6 ftnt b
5:14   OdesSol 15:2
5:22–6:9   Ps-Phoc 175f. ftnt a
6:4   Ps-Phoc 207
6:5   JosAsen 9:1 ftnt a
6:10-20   LAE Apoc 20:2
6:12   AscenIs 1:4
6:12   LAE Vita 21:1 ftnt a
6:12   LAE Vita 28:2

Philippians
2:6-9   OdesSol 41:12
2:9   PrJos Frag A
2:10   AscenIs 10:16
2:12   JosAsen 9:1 ftnt a
3:19   Ps-Phoc 69
3:20   AscenIs 4:13
3:21   AscenIs 4:18
4:19   JosAsen 21:16 ftnt w

4:19   OdesSol 14:10

Colossians
1:13   JosAsen 15:12 ftnt a2
1:15   PrJos Frag A
1:15   HelSynPr 5:20
1:15   HelSynPr 12:10
1:15-20   OdesSol 17:16
1:16   PssSol 2:19 ftnt r
1:16   HelSynPr 4:11
1:16   HelSynPr 12:14
1:16   HelSynPr 12:81
1:16f.   HelSynPr 3:1
1:17   HelSynPr 12:11
1:17   PrJos Frag A
1:21   JosAsen 12:5 ftnt u
1:27   JosAsen 21:16 ftnt w
2:18   AscenIs 7:21
3:18–4:1   Ps-Phoc 175f. ftnt a
3:19   SyrMen 47
3:21   Ps-Phoc 207

1 Thessalonians
1:9   JosAsen 11:10 ftnt c2
1:10   AscenIs 4:13
2:16   PssSol 1:1 ftnt a
2:18   PssSol 2:8 ftnt j
3:13   AscenIs 4:14
3:13   AscenIs 4:16
4:14   AscenIs 4:16
4:16   JosAsen 4:1 ftnt a
4:16   LAE Apoc 22:3
5:15   JosAsen 23:9 ftnt s

2 Thessalonians
1:7   AscenIs 4:14
1:7   AscenIs 4:15
1:8   AscenIs 4:18
2:3   Jub 10:3
2:3f.   PssSol 2:1 ftnt a
2:4   AscenIs 4:7
2:6f.   LAB 51:5 ftnt j
2:8   AscenIs 4:18
2:9   AscenIs 4:9
3:10   Ps-Phoc 153

1 Timothy
1:1   HelSynPr 3:27

1 Timothy (cont.)
1:13	JosAsen 6:7 ftnt s
1:17	HelSynPr 3:1
1:17	HelSynPr 4:29
1:17	HelSynPr 9:4
2:4	HelSynPr 8:5
2:4	HelSynPr 11:8
2:14	LAE Apoc 14:2
3:9	4Bar 7:2 ftnt a
3:15	JosAsen 14:8 ftnt k
4:1	4Bar 7:2 ftnt a
4:12	AscenIs 3:22
5:5	JosAsen 13:2 ftnt b
5:17	HelSynPr 14:6
5:21	JosAsen 16:14 ftnt o
6:7	Ps-Phoc 110f.
6:10	Ah 137
6:13	JosAsen 8:9 ftnt x
6:16	HelSynPr 4:33
6:16	HelSynPr 13:5
6:17	Ps-Phoc 62

2 Timothy
1:10	HelSynPr 5:7
3:8	LAB 47:1 ftnt a
4:17	JosAsen 12:11 ftnt h2

Titus
1:2	OdesSol 3:10 ftnt e
2:12	Aristob Frag 4:8
3:5	JosAsen 8:9 ftnt b2
3:5	HelSynPr 10:8

Hebrews
1:3f.	OdesSol 36:4 ftnt f
1:4	PrJos Frag A
1:6	LAE Vita 14:1 ftnt a
1:14	LAE Vita 14:1 ftnt a
3:7–4:13	JosAsen 8:9 ftnt f2
3:7–4:13	OdesSol 11:12 ftnt n
4:1	OdesSol 25:12
4:12	OdesSol 12:5 ftnt g
4:12	Ps-Phoc 124
6:1	JosAsen 9:2 ftnt c
7:1f.	HelSynPr 12:10
7:26-28	HelSynPr 7:4
9:28	AscenIs 4:13

10:34	JosAsen 12:15 ftnt s2
11:3	JosAsen 12:2 ftnt e
11:3	JosAsen 12:2 ftnt p
11:9	JosAsen 24:14 ftnt p
11:24	EzekTrag 41 ftnt r
11:37	LivPro 1:1 ftnt a
12:22	AscenIs 3:15
12:22	4Bar 5:35
13:2	Ps-Phoc 24-25
13:5	Ps-Phoc 6f.
13:6	OdesSol 7:3 ftnt a
13:15	OdesSol 8:2 ftnt b

James
1:15	LAE Apoc 19:3
1:17	JosAsen 12:15 ftnt q2
1:17	LAE Apoc 36:3 ftnt a
1:19	Ps-Phoc 57
1:21	HelSynPr 11:3
1:23	OdesSol 13:1 ftnt a
1:25	HelSynPr 11:3
2:10	4Mac 5:20
2:11	LAB 11:10 ftnt i
2:23	Jub 19:9
3:5	Ps-Phoc 144 ftnt f
3:6	SyrMen 424
3:11	JosAsen 16:16 ftnt r
4:6	JosAsen 6:8 ftnt t
4:14	HelSynPr 2:10
4:14	Ps-Phoc 117 ftnt a
5:2f.	JosAsen 2:4 ftnt h
5:4	Ps-Phoc 19-21
5:13	PssSol 3:2
5:14	LAE Vita 36:2 ftnt a

1 Peter
1:4	JosAsen 12:15 ftnt q2
2:3	OdesSol 19:1
2:9	Jub 16:19
2:9	JosAsen 8:9 ftnt y
2:12	JosAsen 20:7 ftnt p
2:17	SyrMen 9
2:25	JosAsen 12:5 ftnt u
3:7	JosAsen 24:14 ftnt p
3:9	JosAsen 23:9 ftnt s
3:18-20	AscenIs 9:17
3:19	LAB 32:13 ftnt m

1 Peter (cont.)
3:20   HelSynPr 12:59
3:22   AscenIs 1:4
4:6   LAB 32:13 ftnt m
4:19   JosAsen 13:15 ftnt q
5:5   JosAsen 6:8 ftnt t
5:5   Ah 150 ftnt g
5:8   JosAsen 12:9 ftnt c2

2 Peter
1:11   JosAsen 14:1 ftnt b
2:4   LAE Vita 12:2
2:5   Jub 7:35
2:5   HelSynPr 12:58
2:7   HelSynPr 12:62
2:14   JosAsen 21:21 ftnt c2
2:18   JosAsen 21:21 ftnt c2
3:5   JosAsen 12:2 ftnt j
3:5   JosAsen 12:2 ftnt p
3:6f.   Art Frag 3 (PrEv
                 9.27.37) ftnt x2
3:7   FrgsPoetWrks 6 ftnt d
3:8   Jub 4:30
3:13   Jub 1:29

1 John
1:1f.   JosAsen 12:2 ftnt q
2:18   PssSol 2:1 ftnt a
3:8   JosAsen 12:9 ftnt b2
3:14   JosAsen 8:9 ftnt a2
4:19   OdesSol 3:3
5:16   Jub 21:22

3 John
11   Ps-Phoc 77

Jude
9   LAE Vita 15:3
14   Jub 7:39
14   AscenIs 4:14
14-16   LAE Vita 51:9
15   JosAsen 23:7 ftnt p

Revelation
1:8   Ps-Orph 39
1:8   Aristob Frag 4:5
1:10-12   HistRech 1:3 ftnt h
1:13   JosAsen 14:14 ftnt u

1:13-16   JosAsen 14:9 ftnt q
1:14   JosAsen 5:4 ftnt g
1:16   JosAsen 18:9 ftnt p
1:18   OdesSol 15:9
2:1   AscenIs 3:15
2:7   OdesSol 20:7
2:7   LAE Vita 25:3 ftnt a
2:8   AscenIs 3:15
2:26   JosAsen 12:2 ftnt o
2:28   JosAsen 14:1 ftnt b
3:3   LAE Apoc 19:3 ftnt d
3:7f.   OdesSol 17:9
3:7f.   OdesSol 17:11
3:7f.   OdesSol 42:17
3:12   AscenIs 3:16
3:12   JosAsen 17:6 ftnt e
4:1   JosAsen 10:16 ftnt e2
4:4   AscenIs 7:23
4:6   LAE Vita 29:2 ftnt a
5:1   4Bar 3:10
5:11   JosAsen 16:17 ftnt a2
5:20   Jub 16:19
6:6   JosAsen 8:5 ftnt i
6:8   OdesSol 15:9
7:3   PssSol 15:6
7:17   OdesSol 6:18 ftnt q
7:17   OdesSol 11:6
8:2   LAE Apoc 22:3
8:7-12   LAB 4:3 ftnt q
8:12   LAE Apoc 36:3
9:4   PssSol 15:6
9:7-10   JosAsen 16:18 ftnt c2
9:11   OdesSol 33:1
9:11   OdesSol 38:9
9:15   LAB 4:3 ftnt q
9:18   LAB 4:3 ftnt q
9:20   JosAsen 2:3 ftnt f
9:20f.   JosAsen 9:2 ftnt c
10:1   JosAsen 14:9 ftnt q
10:1   JosAsen 18:9 ftnt p
11:10   JosAsen 11:6 ftnt u
11:15   JosAsen 19:5 ftnt d
12:1   JosAsen 5:5 ftnt k
12:3   OdesSol 22:5
12:7-12   LAE Vita 14:1
12:9   JosAsen 12:9 ftnt b2
12:9   LAE Vita 12:1
12:9   LivPro 12:13

12:17	LivPro 12:13	20:4	AscenIs 4:16
13:4	AscenIs 4:8	20:11-15	AscenIs 4:18
13:8	AscenIs 4:8	20:12	AscenIs 9:22
13:10	SyrMen 18-19	20:12	JosAsen 15:4 ftnt g
13:12	AscenIs 4:8	20:13f.	OdesSol 15:9
13:14	AscenIs 4:9	20:13f.	OdesSol 42:11
13:14f.	AscenIs 4:12	20:15	JosAsen 15:4 ftnt g
14:4	JosAsen 4:7 ftnt n	21:1	OdesSol 6:18 ftnt q
14:11	AscenIs 4:12	21:2	AscenIs 3:16
14:18f.	JosAsen 25:2 ftnt b	21:3	PrJos Frag A
15:2	JosAsen 4:1 ftnt a	21:6	OdesSol 30:1
15:2	LAE Vita 29:2 ftnt a	21:6	OdesSol 6:18 ftnt q
15:6	JosAsen 14:14 ftnt u	21:17	OdesSol 6:18 ftnt q
17:4	JosAsen 2:3 ftnt f	21:19	LAB 26:10 ftnt d
18:19	JosAsen 10:14 ftnt b2	21:20	JosAsen 18:6 ftnt j
19:10	AscenIs 7:21	22:1f.	OdesSol 6:8
19:10	AscenIs 8:6	22:2	LAE Apoc 9:3
19:20	AscenIs 4:9	22:8f.	AscenIs 7:21
19:20	AscenIs 4:15	22:8f.	AscenIs 8:6
19:20	JosAsen 12:11 ftnt k2	22:17	OdesSol 30:2
20:2	JosAsen 12:9 ftnt b2		